# A CONCISE
# EXEGETICAL
# GRAMMAR

## of
## NEW TESTAMENT GREEK

**Fifth Edition**
Revised

*by*
J. Harold Greenlee

WILLIAM B. EERDMANS PUBLISHING COMPANY
GRAND RAPIDS, MICHIGAN

Fifth edition, revised, copyright © 1986 by
Wm. B. Eerdmans Publishing Co., 255 Jefferson Ave. S.E.,
Grand Rapids, Michigan 49503

*First published 1953*
*Revised edition 1958*
*Third edition, revised, 1963*
*Fourth edition, revised, 1979*

**Library of Congress Cataloging-in-Publication Data**

Greenlee, J. Harold (Jacob Harold), 1918-
A concise exegetical grammar of New Testament Greek.

Includes index.
1. Greek language, Biblical — Grammar.   I.  Title.
   PA817.G7      1986      487'.4      86-19711

ISBN 0-8028-0173-0

# Table of Contents

## ETYMOLOGY

# SYNTAX

# PREFACE

This book is intended to meet the needs of students who have completed a course in elementary New Testament Greek. Its purpose is to give a grasp of the principles of grammar which are meaningful in exegesis.

These principles are intentionally presented in concise form. The aim of the book is to be practical, not exhaustive. Minor exceptions to rules are for the most part not presented. For the student who wishes to investigate a point more fully, references to other grammars are given throughout.

Rules given in the book are illustrated by an example from the New Testament with an English translation, plus an example for the student to translate. These latter may be used for class assignments.

I trust that this book, by giving students an unsophisticated presentation of principles, will encourage many in the practice of "rightly dividing the word of truth."

## Preface to the 1986 edition

This new edition is a thoroughgoing revision of the Grammar, based on further years of teaching and research and especially on collaboration with members of Wycliffe Bible Translators / Summer Institute of Linguistics in New Testament translation workshops in various parts of the world.

The present edition includes a new index to over 700 New Testament passages referred to. It also includes a new presentation of the principal parts of the various types of verbs in chart form. Fuller attention has been given to the second conjugation verbs, the optative mood, and third declension nouns. A special section dealing with two important connectives has been added, and the discussion of clues to prominence and emphasis has been expanded.

This new edition utilizes the computer facilities of the Printing Arts Department of the Summer Institute of Linguistics, and I am grateful to Mr. Bob Chaney and his associates for their expertise and help as I keyboarded the book.

I believe students will find this new edition of the Grammar a significant improvement over the previous editions.

The Author
April 1986

The task of exegetical grammar is to enable the interpreter to reproduce in his own mind the exact thought of each given form or expression in the Greek New Testament, and then to express that thought, as nearly as possible, in his own language (Bu 2-5).

# Abbreviations used in this book

**BC**    Beekman, John, and John Callow, *Translating the Word of God*

**BF**    Blass, Friedrich, and Albert Debrunner, *A Greek Grammar of the New Testament*, translated and revised by Robert W. Funk

**Bu**    Burton, Ernest DeWitt, *Syntax of the Moods and Tenses in New Testament Greek*

**Ca**    Carson, D. A., *A Student's Manual of New Testament Greek Accents*

**DM**    Dana, H. E., and Julius R. Mantey, *A Manual Grammar of the Greek New Testament*

**Gl**    Greenlee, J. Harold, *A New Testament Greek Morpheme Lexicon*

**Gr**    Green, Samuel G., *Handbook to the Grammar of the Greek Testament*, rev. ed.

**Ma**    Machen, J. Gresham, *New Testament Greek for Beginners*

**Me**    Metzger, Bruce M., *Lexical Aids for Students of New Testament Greek*

**Mo**    Moulton, James Hope, *Grammar of New Testament Greek. Vol. 1, Prolegomena*

**MH**    Moulton, James Hope, and W. F. Howard, *Grammar of New Testament Greek. Vol. 2, Accidence and Word-Formation*

**Nu**    Nunn, H. P. V., *Short Syntax of New Testament Greek*

**Ro**    Robertson, A. T., *A Grammar of the Greek New Testament in the Light of Historical Research*

**RD**    Robertson, A. T., and W. H. Davis, *A New Short Grammar of the Greek New Testament*

---

References in Green and Blass-Funk are to sections; in all others, to pages. The Greek text is that of the third edition of the UBS text.

# ETYMOLOGY

**I.** The alphabet. Gr §1; Ma 1; DM 20; MH 37

   **A.** Lower case
     α β γ δ ε ζ η θ ι κ λ μ ν ξ ο π ρ σ/ς τ υ φ χ ψ ω

   **B.** Capitals
     Α Β Γ Δ Ε Ζ Η Θ Ι Κ Λ Μ Ν Ξ Ο Π Ρ Σ Τ Υ Φ Χ Ψ Ω

**II.** Vowels and diphthongs. Gr §3; Ma 10-11

   **A.** Vowels: α ε η ι ο υ ω
     Always long: η ω
     Always short: ε ο
     May be long or short: α ι υ

   **B.** Diphthongs

| | | | |
|---|---|---|---|
| αι | αυ | ᾳ | ηυ |
| ει | ευ | ῃ | ωυ |
| οι | ου | ῳ | |
| υι | | | |

   **C.** Definition: A long syllable is a syllable containing a long vowel or
     a diphthong.
     *Exception*: When the diphthongs αι or οι are word-final (i.e., the
     last two letters of a word), they are considered short for purposes
     of accenting when the accent falls on some other syllable.

**III.** Transliteration. Me 3,98-101; Gr §7

   **A.** Single letters
     Most transliterations are obvious (α - *a*, β - *b*, etc.), but the
     following may be mentioned:

     **1.** η - long *e*     υ - *y* (not *u*)
        κ - *c* (usually)   χ - *ch* (not k)
        ξ - x

     **2.** ι usually becomes *i*, but becomes *j* when used as a consonant in
        English (e.g., Ἰησοῦς, 'Jesus').
        Initial ρ, which always has a rough breathing (ῥ-), becomes *rh*
        (e.g., "rhetoric").

   **B.** Diphthongs
     αι - *ae* or *e*     ει - *e* or *i*
     οι - *oe* or *e*     ου - *u*

**IV.** Accents. Ma 13-18 (esp. 14),44-5; Ca (all)

**A.** General rules. Ca 19-23,47-51,149-53

1. The *acute* accent can stand on one of the last three syllables:
   e.g., ἄνθρωπος, ἀνθρώπου, γραφή
   The *circumflex* accent can stand on one of the last two
   syllables: e.g., δῶρον, υἱοῦ
   An acute accent standing on an ultima is replaced by a *grave*
   accent when other words follow in the sentence without
   intervening punctuation: e.g., γραφὴ αὐτοῦ
2. If the ultima is long, the acute accent may stand on one of the
   last two syllables only, and the circumflex on the last
   syllable only: e.g., ἀνθρώπῳ, γραφῆς
3. The circumflex accent may stand on long syllables only: e.g.,
   δῶρα, γραφῶν
4. When the penult (the last syllable but one) is to be accented, if
   it is long and the ultima is short the accent on the penult
   must be a circumflex: e.g., οἶκος

**B.** *Verb* accent is recessive (except in infinitives and participles) --
   i.e., it is placed as far from the ultima as the general rules will
   permit: e.g., λύομεν, πιστεύω

**C.** *Nouns* retain the accent on the same syllable on which it falls in
   the nominative singular, insofar as the general rules permit:
   e.g., ἀπόστολος, ἀποστόλου / δῶρον, δώρου

**D.** *Enclitics* are accented with the word preceding. For purposes of
   accenting, they count in general as additional syllables of the
   preceding word. Specifically--

1. If an enclitic follows a word with an acute on the antepenult or
   a circumflex on the penult, the word preceding the enclitic
   takes an additional acute on the ultima: e.g., ἄνθρωπός μου,
   δῶρόν μου
2. If an enclitic of two syllables follows a word with an acute
   accent on the penult, the enclitic takes its own accent
   (because a word cannot have the same kind of accent on
   successive syllables): e.g., δώρου ἐστίν
3. If an enclitic follows a proclitic or another enclitic, the first of
   the two takes an acute on the ultima: e.g., υἱός μού ἐστιν
   *Exception*: οὐκ ἔστιν
4. If an enclitic follows a word with an accent on the ultima, no
   additional accent is necessary: e.g., γραφῇ ἐστιν, γραφή μου.
   If the accent is an acute, it does not become a grave.
5. An enclitic retains its own accent if it is emphatic or if it
   begins a clause: e.g., ἐστὲ μαθηταί

6. An enclitic's own accent is commonly, but not always, an acute on the ultima (which may become a grave in accordance with the regular rules).

**V.** Rules of contraction and assimilation. Ma 144-5; RD 34-5; Gr §3-5,83; DM 24-5; Gl, Part 2; Ca 24-5

**A.** Vowels

1. A short plus a long of the same vowel form their long: e.g., ε-η form η; ο-ω form ω
2. Two like short vowels form a diphthong: e.g., ε-ε form ει; ο-ο form ου
3. ο or ω contract with α, ε, or η to form ω: e.g., α-ο, α-ω, ο-η, ε-ω form ω
   *Exceptions*: ε-ο or ο-ε form ου
4. α-ε or α-η form long α
5. When a vowel is contracted with a following diphthong which begins with the same vowel, the separate vowel disappears and the diphthong remains: e.g., ο-ου form ου
6. When a vowel is contracted with a diphthong which begins with a different vowel, the separate vowel contracts with the diphthong's first vowel according to the rules. If the diphthong's second vowel is ι, it becomes ι-subscript; otherwise it disappears: e.g., α-ει form ᾳ, α-ου form ω, α-η form ᾳ, ε-ου form ου, ε-η form η
7. Table of contractions for contract verbs

| Stem vowel | \| | Vowel of Termination | | | | | | |
|---|---|---|---|---|---|---|---|---|
| | \| | ω | ο | ου | ε | ει | η | ῃ |
| α | \| | ω | ω | ω | α | ᾳ | α | ᾳ |
| ο | \| | ω | ου | ου | ου | οι | ω | οι |
| ε | \| | ω | ου | ου | ει | ει | η | ῃ |

*Exceptions*: In infinitives, -ά-ειν form -ᾶν, and -ό-ειν form -οῦν

**B.** Consonants

1. π, β, φ plus σ form ψ - (πέμπσω) πέμψω
   κ, γ, χ plus σ form ξ - (ἄγσω) ἄξω
   τ, δ, θ drop out before σ - (πείθσω) πείσω

2. ν followed by π, β, φ becomes μ - (ἐν-βαίνω) ἐμβαίνω
   ν followed by κ, γ, χ becomes γ - (συν-γράφω) συγγράφω
   ν followed by λ, μ, ρ becomes λ, μ, ρ - (ἐν-λείπω) ἐλλείπω
   ν drops out before σ or ζ - (συν-ζάω) συζάω

**3.** Before τ -

β, φ become π - (τέτριβται) τέτριπται

γ, χ      —    κ

τ, δ, θ —    σ

Before δ -

π, φ become β

κ, χ      —    γ

Before θ -

π, β become φ - (ἐπέμπθη) ἐπέμφθη

κ, γ      —    χ

τ, δ, θ —    σ

Before μ -

π, β, φ become μ - (γέγραφμαι) γέγραμμαι

κ, γ, χ    —    γ

τ, δ, θ    —    σ

**4.** π, τ, κ followed by a rough breathing become respectively φ, θ,
χ --e.g., (ἀπ' ὧν) ἀφ' ὧν

**5.** If two consecutive syllables of a word begin with a fricative (φ,
θ, χ), the first usually changes to the corresponding voiceless
stop (π, τ, κ).
Thus θρίξ becomes τριχός (not θριχός) in the gen. sg.; and the
6th prin. part of τίθημι (root θε-) is ἐτέθην (not ἐθέθην).

**6.** A ρ is doubled when a vowel precedes it--e.g., (ἐπι-ρἁπτω)
ἐπιρρἁπτω

**7.** κ becomes ξ before a vowel--e.g., (ἐκ-ἄγω) ἐξἀγω

**VI.** Movable ν. Gr §3h
To facilitate pronunciation, ν is generally added to dative plural
endings in ι and to the third person of verb forms ending in ε or ι
(but not ει) when punctuation or a vowel follows, and sometimes
when μ, τ, δ, or κ follows.

**VII.** Paradigms. Ma 225-51; Gr §9-117

**A.** Declension endings. Ca 27-46,85-92,98-101

**1.** Key to all three declensions: the definite article for the first
and second declensions, and the indefinite pronoun for the
third declension. Ma 230,236; Gr §12-13

**2.** Classes of first declension nouns. Ma 225; Gr §17-20

**a.** Singulars                                                  **b.** Plural of all

| 1) Stem ending: vowel or ρ* | 2) Stem ending: consonant | | 3) Masc. nouns | |
|---|---|---|---|---|
| Nom. -α | -α | -η | -ης | -αι |
| Gen. -ας | -ης | -ης | -ου | -ων |
| Dat. -ᾳ | -ῃ | -ῃ | -ῃ | -αις |
| Acc. -αν | -αν | -ην | -ην | -ας |
| Voc. -α | -α | -η | -α | -αι |
| ἀλήθεια | δόξα | γραφή | προφήτης | |

(*Nom. and acc. sg. long α in both or short α in both)

**3.** Classes of second declension nouns. Ma 226; Gr §21-5

| **a.** Masculine and feminine | | **b.** Neuter | |
|---|---|---|---|
| Singular | Plural | Singular | Plural |
| Nom. -ος | -οι | -ον | -α |
| Gen. -ου | -ων | -ου | -ων |
| Dat. -ῳ | -οις | -ῳ | -οις |
| Acc. -ον | -ους | -ον | -α |
| Voc. -ε | -οι | -ον | -α |
| ἄνθρωπος, ὁ | ὁδός, ἡ | δῶρον, τό | |

**4.** Classes of third declension nouns. Gr §26-31; Gl 259,311-2

**a.** The noun stem is the gen. sg. minus the -ος ending (except for a few irregular nouns).
The nom. sg. is formed from the stem (final stem consonant, vowel, or diphthong may be modified)--

1) By adding -ς to the stem
   E.g., ἰχθύς,-ύος, ὁ    ἔρις,-ιδος, ἡ    οὖς,ὠτός, τό

2) By the stem alone
   E.g., αἰών,-ῶνος, ὁ    πειθώ,-οῦς, ἡ    λέων,-οντος, ὁ

**b.** Third declension endings (often modified by contraction)

| Masculine and Feminine | | | Neuter | |
|---|---|---|---|---|
| Singular | Plural | | Singular | Plural |
| -ς or -__ | -ες | Nom. | -__ | -α |
| -ος | -ων | Gen. | -ος | -ων |
| -ι | -σι | Dat. | -ι | -σι |
| -α or -ν | -ας | Acc. | -__ | -α |
| -ς or -__ | -ες | Voc. | -__ | -α |

**B.** Verb forms. Gr §74-117; BF §65-101; Ca 53-61,70-84,111-4,122-40

**1.** Principal parts of verbs. Ca 146-8
*Note*: All principal part forms are indicative mood, first person singular

| <u>1st</u><br>Pres. act. | <u>2nd</u><br>Fut. act. | <u>3rd</u><br>Aor. act. |
|---|---|---|
| **a.** Regular verb<br>πιστεύω | πιστεύσω | ἐπίστευσα |
| **b.** Deponent verb<br>δέχομαι | δέξομαι | ἐδεξάμην |
| **c.** Contract verbs<br>ἀγαπάω<br>δηλόω<br>λαλέω | ἀγαπήσω<br>δηλώσω<br>λαλήσω | ἠγάπησα<br>ἐδήλωσα<br>ἐλάλησα |
| **d.** Liquid verb<br>κρίνω | (κρινέω) κρινῶ | ἔκρινα |
| **e.** Irregular verb<br>φέρω | οἴσω | ἤνεγκα |
| **f.** Second conjugation verb<br>δίδωμι | δώσω | ἔδωκα |

**2.** Tenses derived from each principal part (except 2nd conjugation verbs)

| <u>1st</u><br>Pres. act.<br>Pres. mid.-pass.<br>Impf. act.<br>Impf. mid.-pass. | <u>2nd</u><br>Fut. act.<br>Fut. mid. | <u>3rd</u><br>Aor. act.<br>Aor. mid. |
|---|---|---|

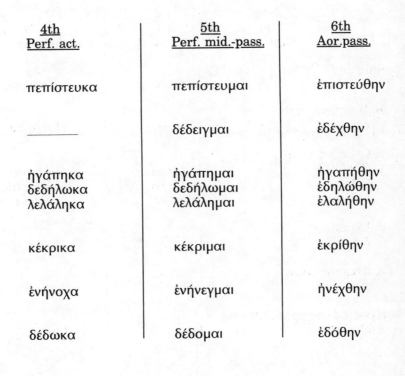

| 4th<br>Perf. act. | 5th<br>Perf. mid.-pass. | 6th<br>Aor.pass. |
|---|---|---|
| πεπίστευκα | πεπίστευμαι | ἐπιστεύθην |
| ——— | δέδειγμαι | ἐδέχθην |
| ἠγάπηκα | ἠγάπημαι | ἠγαπήθην |
| δεδήλωκα | δεδήλωμαι | ἐδηλώθην |
| λελάληκα | λελάλημαι | ἐλαλήθην |
| κέκρικα | κέκριμαι | ἐκρίθην |
| ἐνήνοχα | ἐνήνεγμαι | ἠνέχθην |
| δέδωκα | δέδομαι | ἐδόθην |

All moods are derived from the same principal part
(except 2nd conjugation verbs)

| 4th<br>Perf. act.<br>Pluperf. act. | 5th<br>Perf. mid.-pass.<br>Plup. mid.-pass. | 6th<br>Aor. pass.<br>Fut. pass. |
|---|---|---|

### 3. Verb endings

**a.** The basic endings

|          | Primary Act. |           |
|----------|--------------|-----------|
|          | Sing.        | Pl.       |
| 1st p.   | -ω           | -ομεν     |
| 2nd p.   | -εις         | -ετε      |
| 3rd p.   | -ει          | -ουσι(ν)  |

|          | Primary Mid. |           |
|----------|--------------|-----------|
|          | Sing.        | Pl.       |
| 1st p.   | -ομαι        | -ομεθα    |
| 2nd p.   | -η           | -εσθε     |
| 3rd p.   | -εται        | -ονται    |

**1)** Where used in the indicative mood

Pres. act.
Fut. act.

Pres. mid.-pass.
Fut. mid.
Fut. pass.
Perf. mid.-pass.
 (omit first vowel;
  2nd p. sg. -σαι)

**2)** Where used in the subjunctive mood

Pres. act.
Aor. act.
Aor. pass.
Perf. act.

Pres. mid.-pass.
Aor. mid.

*Note*:
Initial vowel of all endings is lengthened.
Verb stem is not augmented in aorist.
Perf. mid.-pass. must be written peri-
 phrastically, since its verb endings
 have no initial vowel.

|  | Secondary Act. |  |  | Secondary Mid. |
|---|---|---|---|---|
| Sing. | Pl. |  | Sing. | Pl. |
| -ον | -ομεν |  | -ομην | -ομεθα |
| -ες | -ετε |  | -ου | -εσθε |
| -ε(ν) | -ον |  | -ετο | -οντο |

Imperf. act.
1st aor. act.
  (first vowel -α exc.
  3rd p. sg.; 1st p.
  sg. omits -ν)
2nd aor. act.
Aor. pass.
  (first vowel -η; 3rd
  p. pl. -σαν)
Perf. act.
  (first vowel -α exc.
  3rd p. sg.; 1st p.
  sg. omits -ν; 3rd p.
  pl. -ασι)
Pluperf. act.   (first vowel
  becomes -ει;
  3rd p. pl. -εισαν)

Imperf. mid.-pass.
First aor. mid.
  (first vowel -α exc.
  2nd p. sg. ending -ω)
Second aor. mid.
Pluperf. mid.-pass.
  (omit first vowel;
  2nd p. sg. ending -σο)

**b.** Imperative mood endings. Ma 177-80; Ca 64-5

2nd p. sg.--must be learned separately
2nd p. pl.--identical with 2nd p. pl. indicative
3rd p. sg.--change final ε of 2nd p. pl. to ω
3rd p. pl.--add -σαν to 3rd p. sg.

E.g., Pres. act.                    First aor. act.
   Sg.   Pl.                      Sg.   Pl.
  -ε   -ετε      2nd p.  -ον      -ασθε
  -ετω  -ετωσαν   3rd p.  -ασθω    -ασθωσαν

**c.** Infinitive endings and examples
| Pres. act. | -ειν | πιστεύειν |
|---|---|---|
| Pres. mid.-pass. | -εσθαι | πιστεύεσθαι |
| | | |
| First aor. act. | -αι | πιστεῦσαι |
| First aor. mid. | -ασθαι | πιστεύσασθαι |
| Second aor. act. | -εῖν | λιπεῖν |
| Second aor. mid. | -έσθαι | λιπέσθαι |
| Aor. pass. | -ῆναι | πιστευθῆναι |
| | | |
| Perf. act. | -έναι | πεπιστευκέναι |
| Perf. mid.-pass. | -σθαι | πεπιστεῦσθαι |

**d.** Participial endings. Ca 115-9

**1)** All active participles and the aorist passive participle are
declined like third-first-third declension nouns.

Present active
Nom. sg.  -ων      -ουσα    -ον
Gen. sg.  -οντος   -ουσης   -οντος
  E.g., πιστεύων, πιστεύουσα, πιστεῦον

First aorist active
Nom. sg.  -ας      -ασα     -αν
Gen. sg.  -αντος   -ασης    -αντος
*Note*: Final α of nom. sg. is *long* in masculine, *short* in
feminine and neuter.
  E.g., πιστεύσας, πιστεύσασα, πιστεῦσαν

Second aorist active
Nom. sg.  -ών      -οῦσα    -όν
Gen. sg.  -όντος   -ούσης   -όντος
  E.g., λιπών, λιποῦσα, λιπόν

Perfect active
Nom. sg.  -ώς       -υῖα       -ός
Gen. sg.  -ότος     -υίας      -ότος
E.g., λελυκώς, λελυκυῖα, λελυκός

Aorist passive
Nom. sg.  -είς       -εῖσα      -έν
Gen. sg.  -έντος     -είσης     -έντος
E.g., λυθείς, λυθεῖσα, λυθέν

2) All middle participles, and all passives except the aorist, are declined like second-first-second declension adjectives.

Present middle and passive
Nom. sg. -όμενος  -ομένη  -όμενον
E.g., λυόμενος, λυομένη, λυόμενον

First aorist middle
Nom. sg. -άμενος  -αμένη  -άμενον
E.g., λυσάμενος, λυσαμένη, λυσάμενον

Second aorist middle
Nom. sg. -όμενος  -ομένη  -όμενον
E.g., λιπόμενος, λιπομένη, λιπόμενον

Perfect middle and passive
Nom. sg. -μένος  -μένη  -μένον
E.g., λελυμένος, λελυμένη, λελυμένον

4. Notes on second conjugation (-μι) verbs. Gr §64,74ff.,104-7; Ma 200-18,244-51

a. Formation of first principal part: Reduplication + root with lengthened vowel + endings
E.g., τι- θη- -μι

b. Present and imperfect indicative endings differ from those of first conjugation verbs; e.g.,

| Sg. | | Pl. |
|---|---|---|
| δίδωμι | 1st p. | δίδομεν |
| δίδως | 2nd p. | δίδοτε |
| δίδωσι(ν) | 3rd p. | διδόασι(ν) |

c. In forms other than the indicative, the present tenses use the stem of the first principal part (e.g., διδο-), while the aorist drops the reduplication (e.g., δο-); but the endings are identical, with minor exceptions.

| | |
|---|---|
| E.g., pres. act. infinitive | διδόναι |
| aor. act. infinitive | δοῦναι |
| pres. mid.-pass. infinitive | δίδοσθαι |
| aor. mid. infinitive | δόσθαι |
| pres. act. participle | διδούς, διδοῦσα, διδόν |
| aor. act. participle | δούς, δοῦσα, δόν |

**5.** Periphrastic tense formations. BF §352-5; Bu 11,16,36,40

**a.** Consist of the appropriate form of εἰμί plus the present or perfect participle of the desired verb (cf. English "I-am speaking," "We-were being-seen," etc.).

**1)** With the present participle, emphasizing continuation: e.g.,
Present act.: εἶ λύων, 'you are loosing'
Imperfect pass.: ἦν λυόμενος, 'he was being loosed'
Future act.: ἐσόμεθα λύοντες, 'we will be loosing'

**2)** With the perfect participle, emphasizing the resulting state: e.g.,
Perfect act.: εἰμὶ λελυκώς, 'I am in a condition resulting from having loosed'
Pluperfect pass.: ἦτε λελυμένος, 'you were in a condition resulting from having been loosed'
Future perfect act.: ἔσονται λελυκότες, 'they will be in a condition resulting from having loosed'

**b.** The participle is nom. sg. or pl. (except acc. when used with an infinitive), in the required voice.

**c.** Other moods are expressed by changing the mood of εἰμί
E.g., ἵνα ὦμεν λύοντες, 'in order that we may be loosing'; ἔστω λύων, 'let him be loosing.'

**VIII.** Adjectives.

**A.** Attributive and predicate position. Ma 35-6,54

**1.** When used with a noun which has the definite article--

**a.** an adjective or participle in *attributive* position stands in either of the following orders: ὁ καλὸς λόγος or ὁ λόγος ὁ καλός, 'the good word.'

**b.** an adjective or participle in *predicate* position stands in either of the following orders: καλὸς ὁ λόγος or ὁ λόγος καλός, 'the word is good.'

2. When used with a noun which does *not* have the definite article--
   an adjective or participle may either precede or follow the noun, normally has no article, and may be either attributive or predicate as the context permits: καλὸς λόγος or λόγος καλός, 'a good word' or 'a word is good.'

**B.** Forms of adjectives. Ma 230-5; Gr §33-41; Gl 295-9; Ca 43-5,93-5,102-5

1. Second-first-second declension.
   Masculine and neuter, 2nd declension; feminine, 1st declension.

   **a.** The vowel of the fem. sg. endings is long α if the stem ends in a vowel or ρ, otherwise η
   E.g., δίκαιος, δικαία, δίκαιον   ἀγαθός, ἀγαθή, ἀγαθόν

   **b.** The neut. nom. and acc. sing. of a few adjectives is -o instead of -ον
   E.g., ἄλλος,-η,-ο

   **c.** Participles of the middle voice, and all passives except the aorist, are declined like this class
   E.g., λυόμενος, λυομένη, λυόμενον

2. Second declension.
   Feminine endings are identical with the masculine
   E.g., αἰώνιος,-ιον   ἄδικος,-ον

3. Third-first-third declension.
   Masculine and neuter, 3rd declension; feminine, 1st declension.

   **a.** The vowel of the fem. sg. endings is always short α
   E.g., πᾶς, πᾶσα, πᾶν

   **b.** All active participles and the aorist passive participle are declined like this class; e.g., λύων, λύουσα, λῦον.
   However, the fem. gen. sg. always has a circumflex accent on the ultima, like nouns: e.g., λυουσῶν.

4. Third declension.
   Feminine endings are identical with the masculine
   E.g., ἀληθής,-ές

**C.** Comparison of adjectives. Gr §42-7; Ma 193; BF §60-1; Gl 287-8,312-3; Ca 108-9

1. Comparative degree: stem + -τερος,-α,-ον
   Superlative degree: stem + -τατος,-η,-ον
   E.g., ἰσχυρός, ἰσχυρότερος, ἰσχυρότατος

2. Comparative degree: stem (possibly modified) + -ίων,-ίων,-ίον
   (third declension)
   Superlative degree: stem (possibly modified) + -ιστος,-ίστη,
   -ιστον
   E.g., μέγας, μείζων, μέγιστος

3. The comparison of many adjectives is irregular.
   E.g., ἀγαθός, κρείσσων, κράτιστος

**IX.** Pronouns. Gr §53-62; Ma 235-7; MH 178-82; BF §64; Ca 56-7, 63-4,67-9,95-6

**A.** Personal

I, my, me: ἐγώ, ἐμοῦ (μου), ἐμοί (μοι), ἐμέ (με)
we, our, us: ἡμεῖς, ἡμῶν, ἡμῖν, ἡμᾶς

you, your (sg.): σύ, σοῦ (σου), σοί (σοι), σέ (σε)
you, your (pl.): ὑμεῖς, ὑμῶν, ὑμῖν, ὑμᾶς

he, she, it, him, her, etc.: αὐτός,-ή,-ό
they, their, them: αὐτοί,-αί,-ά

**B.** Possessive
The genitive of the above personal pronouns: μου, σου, etc.

Possessive adjectives:
my: ἐμός, ἐμή, ἐμόν          our: ἡμέτερος,-α,-ον
your (sg.): σός, σή, σόν     your (pl.): ὑμέτερος,-α,-ον
one's own (his, their, etc.; emphatic possessive adj.): ἴδιος,-α,-ον

**C.** Intensive
(I) myself, (the children) themselves, etc.; "-self" in apposition
with a noun or pronoun in any case: αὐτός in predicate position
E.g., ὁ υἱὸς αὐτός, 'the son himself'; βλέπομεν τοὺς ἀποστόλους
αὐτούς, 'We see the apostles themselves.'

**D.** Reflexive
"-self" forms in the predicate referring back to the same person in
the subject

E.g., "I see myself," "A man knows himself"; declined like 2nd-1st-2nd declension adjectives. (Not used in nom.; forms given are gen.)

myself: ἐμαυτοῦ,-ῆς,-οῦ
yourself (sg.): σεαυτοῦ,-ῆς,-οῦ
him-, her-, itself: ἑαυτοῦ,-ῆς,-οῦ
our-, your- (pl.), themselves: pl. of ἑαυτοῦ,-ῆς,-οῦ

The genitive is sometimes used as an emphatic possessive pronoun.
E.g., Mt. 8:22, τοὺς ἑαυτῶν νεκρούς, 'their own dead'.

**E.** Reciprocal
"one another, each other." Plural only; not used in nom.
Declined like 2nd-1st-2nd declension adjectives; gen. pl., ἀλλήλων.
E.g., Jn. 13:34, ἵνα ἀγαπᾶτε ἀλλήλους, 'that you should love one another'.
Sometimes expressed by the reflexive pronoun.
E.g., Jn. 12:19, εἶπαν πρὸς ἑαυτούς, 'they said to one another'.

**F.** Relative
"who, which." ὅς, ἥ, ὅ, declined like 2nd-1st-2nd declension adjectives.

**G.** Interrogative
"who? which?" τίς, τί, 3rd declension. Acute accent on first syllable, which never changes to grave.

**H.** Indefinite
"someone, something." τις, τι, 3rd declension, enclitic. When the accent is required, it falls on the final syllable; e.g., τινές, τινῶν.

**I.** Indefinite relative.
"whoever, whatever." ὅστις, ἥτις, ὅτι, both syllables declined; e.g., οἵτινες. Sometimes used without indefinite sense, sometimes with qualitative sense.

**J.** Demonstrative
This: οὗτος, αὕτη, τοῦτο
That: ἐκεῖνος, ἐκείνη, ἐκεῖνο
Declined like 2nd-1st-2nd declension adjectives.

**X.** Numerals. Gr §1,48-52; MH 167-69; BF §63; Ca 105-6

Greek letters are used as numerals, in a system more nearly resembling the Roman system than the Arabic, although differing from both. Because some letters were dropped from the Greek

alphabet in very ancient times, three additional symbols are
supplied as numerals: ϛ (*stigma*), 6; ϙ (*koppa*), 90; and ϡ (*sampi*),
900.
When Greek letters are used as numerals, an acute accent follows
the final letter. An inverted acute accent placed under a letter
multiplies that letter's value by one thousand.

| Symbol | Value | Name |
|---|---|---|
| α´ | 1 | εἷς, μία, ἕν |
| β´ | 2 | δύο |
| γ´ | 3 | τρεῖς, τρία |
| δ´ | 4 | τέσσαρες,-α |
| ε´ | 5 | πέντε |
| ϛ´ | 6 | ἕξ, handwritten symbol |
| ζ´ | 7 | ἑπτά |
| η´ | 8 | ὀκτώ |
| θ´ | 9 | ἐννέα |
| ι´ | 10 | δέκα |
| κ´ | 20 | εἴκοσι(ν) |
| λ´ | 30 | τριάκοντα |
| μ´ | 40 | τεσσαράκοντα |
| ν´ | 50 | πεντήκοντα |
| ξ´ | 60 | ἑξήκοντα |
| ο´ | 70 | ἑβδομήκοντα |
| π´ | 80 | ὀγδοήκοντα |
| ϙ´ | 90 | ἐνενήκοντα, handwritten symbol |
| ρ´ | 100 | ἑκατόν |
| ς´ | 200 | διακόσιοι |
| τ´ | 300 | τριακόσιοι |
| υ´ | 400 | τετρακόσιοι |
| φ´ | 500 | πεντακόσιοι |
| χ´ | 600 | ἑξακόσιοι |
| ψ´ | 700 | ἑπτακόσιοι |
| ω´ | 800 | ὀκτακόσιοι |
| ϡ´ | 900 | ἐνακόσιοι, handwritten symbol |
| ͵α | 1000 | χίλιοι |
| ͵ι | 10000 | μύριοι |
| ͵αα´ | 1001 | χίλιοι καὶ εἷς |
| ͵αρ´ | 1100 | χίλιοι καὶ ἑκατόν |
| ια´ | 11 | ἕνδεκα |
| ιβ´ | 12 | δώδεκα |
| κα´ | 21 | εἴκοσι καὶ εἷς |

εἷς is declined according to the third-first-third declensions. The
genitive is ἑνός, μιᾶς, ἑνός.
δύο is indeclinable except for the dative form δυσί(ν).
τρεῖς and τέσσαρες are declined as third declension plurals.
The numerals 5 to 200 are indeclinable.

διακόσιοι (200) and the higher hundreds and thousands are declined as second-first-second declension plurals.

*Examples*: Identify the following numbers: νη´   τλγ´

Write the following in Greek symbols: 77    144    666

**XI. Adverbs.** Ma 194; Gr §126-34; Me 110; BF §102-6; Ca 120

**A.** Some correlative adverbs

|  | Demonstrative | | Relative | Interrogative | Indefinite |
|---|---|---|---|---|---|
| Time | τότε | νῦν | ὅτε | πότε; | ποτε |
|  | then | now | when | when? | sometime |
| Place | ὧδε | αὐτοῦ | οὖ | ποῦ; | που |
|  | here | here, | where | where? | somewhere |
|  |  | there |  |  |  |
| Manner | οὕτω(ς) |  | ὡς | πῶς; | πως |
|  | thus, so |  | as | how? | somehow |

**XII. Word formation.** Me 53-63; Gr §139-59; BF §108-24; Gl (all)

**A.** Prefixes. Gl 145-48,187-8; Part 2

**1.** Prepositions as prefixes. See pp. 29-44 below.

**2.** Other prefixes. See also Gl 145-8

| ἀ- | not | ἄγνοια, ἡ, ignorance |
|---|---|---|
| δυσ- | mis-, bad | δύσκολος,-ον, difficult |
| εὐ- | well, good | εὐαγγέλιον, τό, good news, Gospel |

**B.** Compounds formed by two or more words. Gr §148; Me 62; Gl 149-259

E.g., καρδιογνώστης (καρδία, γνώστης), heart-knower
θεόπνευστος (θεός, πνέω), God-breathed

**C.** Suffixes. Gl 259-328

**1.** Principal noun-forming suffixes (see others in Gl, Part 2)

**a.** Action, process: -σις,-σεως, ἡ   3rd decl.
**b.** Action, state: -μος, ὁ   2nd decl.
**c.** Agent: -τωρ,-τορος, ὁ   3rd decl.
**d.** Agent, citizen of: -ευς,-εως, ὁ   3rd decl.
**e.** Agent, instrument: -της,-του, ὁ   2nd decl.

**f.** Agent, proper name: -ης,-ου, ὁ    2nd decl.
**g.** Diminutive: -ιον, τό    2nd decl.
          -άριον, τό    2nd decl.
**h.** Feminine indicator, diminutive, object: -ις,-ιδος, ἡ    3rd decl.
**i.** Instrument: -τρον, τό    2nd decl.
**j.** Object, result of action: -μα,-ματος, τό    3rd decl.
**k.** Object, concept: -ος,-ους, τό    3rd decl.
**l.** A person from: -ίτης,-ου, ὁ    2nd decl.
**m.** Place: -τήριον, τό    2nd decl.
**n.** Quality: -οσύνη, ἡ    1st decl.
        -(ό)της,-(ό)τητος, ἡ    3rd decl.
        -εια, ἡ    1st decl.
        -εία, ἡ    1st decl.
**o.** Quality, proper name: -ία, ἡ    1st decl.

Examples:

| | |
|---|---|
| **a.** κρίσις,-σεως, ἡ | a judging |
| **b.** βαθμός, ὁ | a standing |
| **c.** ῥήτωρ,-τορος, ὁ | an orator, a speaker |
| **d.** ἱερεύς,-έως, ὁ | a priest |
| **e.** μαθητής,-τοῦ, ὁ | a disciple, a learner |
| **f.** τελώνης,-ου, ὁ | a tax-collector |
| **g.** παιδίον, τό | a small child |
|    κυνάριον, τό | a little dog |
| **h.** Ἑλληνίς,-ίδος, ἡ | a Greek woman |
| **i.** λύτρον, τό | a ransom |
| **j.** γράμμα,-ματος, τό | a letter (of the alphabet) |
| **k.** κράτος,-ους, τό | strength |
| **l.** Ἰσραηλίτης,-ου, τό | an Israelite |
| **m.** θυσιαστήριον, τό | an altar of sacrifice |
| **n.** ἁγιωσύνη, ἡ | holiness |
|    τελειότης,-τητος, ἡ | perfection, completeness |
|    ἀλήθεια, ἡ | truth |
|    παιδεία, ἡ | instruction |
| **o.** ἀδικία, ἡ | unrighteousness |

*Note*: Suffixes are sometimes extended to other meanings; e.g., κρίσις sometimes means "judgment" (the result) instead of "judging" (the process). Also, some nouns in -ιον are not diminutives but substantivized from the neuter of adjectives in -ιος,-ια,-ιον; e.g., τὸ δαιμόνιον (from δαιμόνιος,-α,-ον).

**2.** Principal adjective-forming suffixes (see others in Gl, Part 2)

**a.** Attribute, locality, related to: -ιος,(-ια),-ιον
**b.** Characteristics of: -ικος,-ίκη,-ικον

    **c.** Made of: -ινος,-ίνη,-ινον
    **d.** From the place of, characteristics of: -νος,-νη,-νον
    **e.** Fitness or ability: -ιμος,-ιμον
    **f.** Quality of, tendency: -μων,-μον
    **g.** Quality of: -ος,(-α or -η),-ον
                    -ης,-ες
                    -υς,-εια,-υ
    **h.** Possibility or actuality of: -τος,-τη,-τον
    **i.** Obligation or intention: -τέος,-τέα,-τέον
    **j.** Hundreds indicator: -κόσιοι,-κόσιαι,-κόσια

Examples:

| | |
|---|---|
| **a.** οὐράνιος,-ον | heavenly |
| **b.** βασιλικός,-ή,-όν | royal |
| **c.** λίθινος,-η,-ον | made of stone |
| **d.** Ναζαρηνός,-ή,-όν | from Nazareth |
| **e.** χρήσιμος,-ον | useful |
| **f.** ἐλεήμων,-μον | merciful |
| **g.** καλός,-ή,-όν | good |
|    ἀληθής,-ές | true |
|    βαρύς,-εία,-ύ | heavy |
| **h.** ἀγαπητός,-ή,-όν | beloved |
| **i.** βλητέος,-α,-ον | must be put |
| **j.** πεντακόσιοι,-αι,-α | five hundred |

**3.** Principal verb-forming suffixes (see also Gl, Part 2)

    **a.** Generally, to do, to be: -αζω, -ανω, -αω, -ευω, -εω, -ζω, -ιζω, -μι, -σσω, -ω
    E.g., δουλεύω, to be a slave

    **b.** Generally, to cause to be: -αινω, -οω, -υνω
    E.g., δουλόω, to enslave, to cause to be a slave

**4.** Principal adverb-forming suffixes (see also Gl, Part 2)

    **a.** Many adverbs of manner: -ως, added to adjective stem
    E.g., καλῶς, well; ἀξίως, worthily

    **b.** Some adverbs of manner or location: -η
    E.g., εἰκῇ, in vain; πεζῇ, on foot

    **c.** From a place: -θεν
    E.g., ἐντεῦθεν, from here

**D.** Example of compounds and family of words. Gr §149; Me 65-94; Gl 149-259

κρίνω, I judge
κρίσις, the process of judging, judgment
κρίμα, the result of judging, sentence
κριτής, one who judges, a judge
ἀνακρίνω, I examine
ἀποκρίνομαι, I answer
διακρίνω, I distinguish
κατακρίνω, I condemn
ὑποκρίτης, an actor, a hypocrite
ἀδιάκριτος, impartial, not subject to distinction or hesitation

# SYNTAX

**I. THE ARTICLE.** Gr §193-234; RD 275-83; DM 137-53; BF §249-76

**A.** General rule

**1.** Nouns *with* the definite article are either *definite* or *generic*.

    **a.** Definite. Jn. 1:1, Ἐν ἀρχῇ ἦν ὁ λόγος, In the beginning was *the word*. Jn. 1:5, τὸ φῶς.

    **b.** Generic. Jn. 2:25, ἵνα τις μαρτυρήσῃ περὶ τοῦ ἀνθρώπου, that anyone should testify concerning *man*. Jn. 10:10, ὁ κλέπτης.

**2.** Nouns *without* the definite article are either *indefinite* or *qualitative*.

    **a.** Indefinite. Jn. 1:6, Ἐγένετο ἄνθρωπος, There came *a man*. Jn. 1:19, ἱερεῖς.

    **b.** Qualitative. Jn. 1:4, ἐν αὐτῷ ζωὴ ἦν, In him there was *life*. Jn. 1:14, σάρξ.

**B.** Corollaries of the general rule
    *Note*: If a noun has the definite article but no modifier, a corollary of, or exception to, the general rule *must* apply; otherwise, they may or may not apply.

    **1.** A separate article preceding various words, phrases, or clauses implies an understood noun agreeing with the article; it makes a substantive expression.

        **a.** With an adverb: ἡ ἐπαύριον (ἡμέρα), the following (day).

        **b.** With a genitive phrase: οἱ τοῦ Ἰωάννου, the (sons/disciples) of John.

        **c.** With a clause: τὸ εἰ δύνῃ, the "If you are able" statement.

    **2.** With the verbs εἰμί and γίνομαι, a noun with the article is normally the subject and a noun without the article is

normally the predicate. Jn. 1:1, θεὸς ἦν ὁ λόγος, the Word
was God.

However, if the predicate is definite, generic, or identical with
the subject, the predicate will have the article also. Jn. 1:4, ἡ
ζωὴ ἦν τὸ φῶς, the life was the light.

If the subject is indefinite or qualitative, it will not have the
article. Jn. 1:4, ἐν αὐτῷ ζωὴ ἦν, in him life was.

3. The article is used with *monadic* nouns (objects of which for
the writer there is but one); e.g., "heaven," "earth," etc.
(Sometimes, however, monadic nouns follow the rule
governing proper nouns; see C.5. below.) Jn. 3:31, ἐκ τῆς γῆς,
from the earth. Jn. 3:31, ἐκ τοῦ οὐρανοῦ.

4. The article is used with nouns which are *set apart* as a special
member of their class. Jn. 3:14, ἐν τῇ ἐρήμῳ, in the desert
(the particular desert in that area). Jn. 5:39, τὰς γραφάς,
the Scriptures (a special group of "writings"). Mt. 12:41, τῇ
κρίσει.

5. (Generic use) The article is used with nouns *typical* of their
class, in proverbs, general truths, etc. Lk. 10:7, ἄξιος γὰρ ὁ
ἐργάτης τοῦ μισθοῦ αὐτοῦ, for the (typical) workman is
worthy of his wages. Jn. 10:10, ὁ κλέπτης.

6. The article is used for renewed mention of a noun. Jn. 4:40,43,
ἔμεινεν ἐκεῖ δύο ἡμέρας . . . . Μετὰ δὲ τὰς δύο ἡμέρας . . . ,
he remained there two days . . . . And after *the* two days . . .

7. The article is used with abstract nouns objectified or
personified. Jn. 1:17, ἡ χάρις καὶ ἡ ἀλήθεια . . . ἐγένετο,
grace and truth came. (Contrast χάριν ἀντὶ χάριτος, without
articles, immediately preceding.) Ac. 28:4, ἡ δίκη.

8. When possession is obvious, the possessive pronoun is
sometimes omitted; the article, by making the noun definite,
implies possession also. Jn. 7:30, οὐδεὶς ἐπέβαλεν ἐπ᾽ αὐτὸν
τὴν χεῖρα, no one put *the* (i.e., *his*) hand upon him. Jn. 3:17,
τὸν υἱὸν.

9. When a demonstrative pronoun is used with a noun, the noun
*must* have the article and the demonstrative pronoun *must*
stand in *predicate* position. Jn. 7:36, τίς ἐστιν ὁ λόγος οὗτος;
What is this word?

When there is no article, the demonstrative must be considered
as standing apart from the noun. Jn. 6:42, οὐχ οὗτός ἐστιν
Ἰησοῦς ὁ υἱὸς Ἰωσήφ; Is not this man Jesus the son of
Joseph? (Not 'This Jesus is . . .') Jn. 18:30, Εἰ μὴ ἦν οὗτος
κακὸν ποιῶν.

10. When the nominative case is used for the vocative, the noun takes the article. Jn. 19:3, χαῖρε ὁ βασιλεὺς τῶν 'Ιουδαίων, Hail, King of the Jews! Jn. 20:28, ὁ κύριος . . . ὁ θεός.

11. Granville Sharp's rule: When the article is used before the first member only of a series, the members are to be considered as a connected whole. When the article is used before each member, each is to be considered separately. Eph. 3:18, τὸ πλάτος καὶ μῆκος καὶ ὕψος καὶ βάθος, the width and length and height and depth (as one image). Lk. 12:11, ἐπὶ τὰς συναγωγὰς καὶ τὰς ἀρχὰς καὶ τὰς ἐξουσίας, to the synagogues and the rulers and the authorities (considered separately). Jn. 7:45, τοὺς ἀρχιερεῖς καὶ Φαρισαίους. Eph. 4:11, τοὺς μὲν ἀποστόλους, τοὺς δὲ προφήτας, τοὺς δὲ εὐαγγελιστάς, τοὺς δὲ ποιμένας καὶ διδασκάλους (the latter two considered together).

C. Exceptions to the general rule

1. When a predicate noun precedes the verb εἰμί it normally does *not* have the article, even if it is definite. Jn. 9:5, φῶς εἰμι τοῦ κόσμου, I am *the* light of the world (cf. Jn. 8:12, 'Εγώ εἰμι τὸ φῶς τοῦ κόσμου). Mt. 14:33, 'Αληθῶς θεοῦ υἱὸς εἶ. However, Mk. 15:39, υἱὸς θεοῦ ἦν, may be either "the son of God" or "a son of God," since a Roman soldier is speaking.

2. In some idiomatic phrases, a modifying word or phrase may make a noun definite even though the noun has no article. (The context must clearly show that the noun is definite.) The defining phrase is usually also without the article. Jn. 12:13, ἐν ὀνόματι κυρίου, in *the* name of *the* Lord (not 'in a name of a lord'). Ac. 11:21, χεὶρ κυρίου.

3. In some prepositional phrases which are idioms of time, place, etc., the object of the preposition has no article but is nevertheless definite (cf. the English phrase "at home" and the British phrase "in hospital"). Jn.1:1,2, ἐν ἀρχῇ, in the beginning. Lk. 15:25, ἐν ἀγρῷ.

4. Nouns in the vocative case are definite, but have no article. Jn. 4:15, κύριε, δός μοι τοῦτο τὸ ὕδωρ, Sir, give me this water. Jn. 2:4, γύναι.

5. (Partial exception) Proper names of persons and places, and divine names and titles (e.g., θεός, ἅγιον πνεῦμα) are definite in themselves; they may or may not take the article. Jn. 1:43-44, τὴν Γαλιλαίαν . . . Φίλιππον . . . ὁ 'Ιησοῦς . . . ὁ Φίλιππος . . . Βηθσαιδά . . . , Galilee . . . Philip . . . Jesus . . . Philip . . . Bethsaida. Jn. 3:2, ἀπὸ θεοῦ ἐλήλυθας, you have

come from God. Jn. 3:2, ἐὰν μὴ ᾖ ὁ θεὸς μετ' αὐτοῦ, unless
God is with him. Jn. 2:1, Κανὰ τῆς Γαλιλαίας.

However, when θεός or πνεῦμα ἅγιον has the article the
*person* (i.e., *who* he is) is usually being thought of; and when
there is no article his *nature* (i.e., *what* he is) or his activity is
usually being thought of. Jn. 1:1, ὁ λόγος ἦν πρὸς τὸν θεόν,
καὶ θεὸς ἦν ὁ λόγος, the Word was with God (the Father),
and the Word was deity (i.e., of the nature of God).

*Note*: In the few N.T. instances in which θεός refers to "a god,"
this special rule does not apply; e.g., 2 Cor. 4:4, ὁ θεὸς τοῦ
αἰῶνος τούτου, the god of this age.

**D.** The article preceding μέν or δέ with no expressed or understood
substantive is actually an archaic pronoun conveying slight
emphasis; e.g., Jn. 7:12, οἱ μὲν ἔλεγον, *some* were saying.

In narrative, the article with δέ indicates a change of speaker. Jn.
4:31-32, ἠρώτων αὐτὸν οἱ μαθηταὶ . . . . ὁ δὲ εἶπεν, the
disciples were asking him . . . , but he said. Ac. 14:4, καὶ οἱ μὲν
ἦσαν . . . . οἱ δὲ . . . . Jn. 5:10-11, ἔλεγον οὖν οἱ Ἰουδαῖοι . . . . ὁ
δὲ ἀπεκρίθη . . . .

**II.** CASES (not including cases after prepositions). BF §143-202; Gr
§241-87

**A.** Nominative

1. Subject of finite verb. Jn. 1:4, ἡ ζωὴ ἦν τὸ φῶς τῶν
   ἀνθρώπων, *the life* was the light of men. Jn. 1:2, οὗτος.

2. Predicate of εἰμί and γίνομαι. Jn. 1:4, ἡ ζωὴ ἦν τὸ φῶς τῶν
   ἀνθρώπων, the life was *the light* of men.

3. Sometimes used for the vocative (must have the article). Jn.
   19:3, χαῖρε ὁ βασιλεὺς τῶν Ἰουδαίων, Hail, *King* of the
   Jews! Jn. 20:28, ὁ κύριός μου καὶ ὁ θεός μου.

**B.** Vocative
   Used in direct address, with or without the interjection ὦ. Jn.
   19:26, γύναι, ἴδε, Woman, behold. Ac. 1:1, ὦ Θεόφιλε, O
   Theophilus. Jn. 4:15, κύριε.

**C.** Genitive. BC 249-66

1. Possessive. Mt. 9:6, τὸν οἶκόν σου, your house (the house that
   belongs to you). Mk. 10:50, τὸ ἱμάτιον αὐτοῦ.

2. Role relationship (father, enemy, servant, etc.). Jn. 3:29, ὁ
   φίλος τοῦ νυμφίου, the friend of the bridegroom. Jn. 4:20, οἱ
   πατέρες ἡμῶν.

3. Source or author. Ro. 4:13, διὰ δικαιοσύνης πίστεως, through the righteousness which has its source in faith. Ro. 15:4, τῶν γραφῶν.

4. Subjective. Modifies a noun of action, expressing the *doer* of that action. Jn. 2:6, κατὰ τὸν καθαρισμὸν τῶν ᾽Ιουδαίων, for the cleansing-rites which the Jews performed. Ac. 1:22, ᾽Ιωάννου.

5. Objective. Modifies a noun of action, expressing the *receiver* of that action. Jn. 3:1, ἄρχων τῶν ᾽Ιουδαίων, one who ruled over the Jews. Jn. 3:10, ὁ διδάσκαλος τοῦ ᾽Ισραήλ.

6. Material. Mk. 2:21, ἐπίβλημα ῥάκους ἀγνάφου, a patch made of unshrunk cloth. Mk. 14:3, νάρδου.

7. Contents. Jn. 2:7, γεμίσατε τὰς ὑδρίας ὕδατος, Fill the water-jars *with water*. Mk. 14:3, μύρου.

8. Partitive. Expresses the *whole* of which the noun it modifies is a part:

a. As a *named part* of the person or thing. Jn. 20:25, ἐν ταῖς χερσὶν αὐτοῦ, in his hands (i.e., in the hands *of him*). Jn. 11:2, τοὺς πόδας αὐτοῦ.

b. As a *portion or fraction* of the whole. Jn. 2:11, ἀρχὴν τῶν σημείων, the beginning of the miracle-signs. Jn. 4:39, πολλοὶ . . . . τῶν Σαμαριτῶν.

c. As a *characteristic* of the person or thing. Jn. 1:14, τὴν δόξαν αὐτοῦ, his glory. Mt. 5:20, ὑμῶν ἡ δικαιοσύνη.

9. Locative. The genitive gives the location of the noun it modifies. Jn. 2:1, ἐν Κανὰ τῆς Γαλιλαίας, in Cana of (i.e., which is located in) Galilee. Jn. 4:5, εἰς πόλιν τῆς Σαμαρείας.

10. Measure. The genitive names the item which is being measured. Lk. 16:6, ῾Εκατὸν βάτους ἐλαίου, a hundred measures of olive oil. Mk. 8:19, πόσους κοφίνους κλασμάτων.

11. Appositive. (Cf. English "the city *of* Dallas.") Eph. 6:14, τὸν θώρακα τῆς δικαιοσύνης, the breastplate which is righteousness. Eph. 6:16, τὸν θυρεὸν τῆς πίστεως. Eph. 6:17, τὴν περικεφαλαίαν τοῦ σωτηρίου.
*Note*: Apposition is more commonly expressed by using the same case for both nouns, as in English; e.g., Jn. 1:23, ᾽Ησαΐας ὁ προφήτης, Isaiah the prophet.

**12.** Comparative. The first member of the comparison takes its normal case; the second member is in the genitive case. Jn. 4:12, μὴ σὺ μείζων εἶ τοῦ πατρὸς ἡμῶν ᾿Ιακώβ; Are *you* greater than our *father* Jacob? Jn. 13:16, δοῦλος μείζων τοῦ κυρίου . . . . ἀπόστολος μείζων τοῦ πέμψαντος αὐτόν. Jn. 21:15, ἀγαπᾷς με πλέον τούτων;

Comparison may also be expressed by ἤ, 'than', followed by the second member in the same case as the first member. Jn. 3:19, ἠγάπησαν οἱ ἄνθρωποι μᾶλλον τὸ σκότος ἢ τὸ φῶς, men loved the darkness rather than the light. Lk. 9:13, Οὐκ εἰσὶν . . . πλεῖον ἢ ἄρτοι πέντε.

**13.** Price, equivalent, or penalty. Jn. 12:5, διὰ τί τοῦτο τὸ μύρον οὐκ ἐπράθη τριακοσίων δηναρίων; Why was this ointment not sold for (the price of) 300 denarii? Lk. 24:20, εἰς κρίμα θανάτου, to the sentence of death. Mt. 10:29, ἀσσαρίου.

**14.** Time within which. Jn. 3:2, οὗτος ἦλθεν πρὸς αὐτὸν νυκτός, This man came to him during the night. Lk. 18:7, ἡμέρας καὶ νυκτός.

**15.** Qualitative. The genitive gives a quality or characteristic of the noun to which it is related. It includes abstract nouns used with adjectival force. Ga. 6:1, ἐν πνεύματι πραΰτητος, in a spirit of gentleness (i.e., with a gentle spirit). Lk. 18:6, ὁ κριτὴς τῆς ἀδικίας.

**16.** Qualified (the reverse of 15). The genitive noun is the concept being described, and the noun modified by it is the qualifier. Eph. 1:7, τὸ πλοῦτος τῆς χάριτος, the riches of the grace (i.e., 'the rich grace', not 'the gracious riches'). Ro. 9:23, τὸν πλοῦτον τῆς δόξης.

**17.** Predicate of various verbs, and with related adjectives:

**a.** Sense perceptions, memory, etc. Jn. 15:20, μνημονεύετε τοῦ λόγου, Remember the word. Jn. 20:17, μή μου ἅπτου.
*Note*: The verb ἀκούω normally takes the accusative of the *thing* heard and the genitive of the *person* heard. Jn. 3:8, τὴν φωνὴν αὐτοῦ ἀκούεις, you hear its sound. Jn. 1:37, ἤκουσαν οἱ δύο μαθηταὶ αὐτοῦ λαλοῦντος, the two disciples heard him speaking.

**b.** Partaking, attaining (a part of). Jn. 8:52, οὐ μὴ γεύσηται θανάτου, he will by no means taste (of) death. Lk. 20:35, τοῦ αἰῶνος ἐκείνου τυχεῖν.

**c. Fullness, lack, etc.** Ac. 13:52, οἵ τε μαθηταὶ ἐπληροῦντο χαρᾶς καὶ πνεύματος ἁγίου, and the disciples were filled with joy and the Holy Spirit. Ro. 3:23, πάντες . . . ὑστεροῦνται τῆς δόξης τοῦ θεοῦ.

**d. Accusing, etc.** Jn. 5:45, μὴ δοκεῖτε ὅτι ἐγὼ κατηγορήσω ὑμῶν, Do not think that I will accuse you. Ac. 19:40, ἐγκαλεῖσθαι στάσεως.

**e. Separation.** Ac. 27:43, ἐκώλυσεν αὐτοὺς τοῦ βουλήματος, he restrained them from the plan. Eph. 2:12, ἀπηλλοτριωμένοι τῆς πολιτείας.

**18. General relationship.** Genitives which fit none of the above categories, but which are related to the modified noun in some way, which must be specified for each instance. Jn. 5:29, ἀνάστασιν ζωῆς . . . ἀνάστασιν κρίσεως, a resurrection which results in life . . . a resurrection which results in judgment. Jn. 7:35, εἰς τὴν διασπορὰν τῶν Ἑλλήνων, into the dispersion of the Greeks (i.e., to the dispersed Jews who live among the Greeks).

**19. Genitive absolute.** A noun or pronoun modified by a participle, (usually) grammatically independent of the rest of the clause. Jn. 2:3, καὶ ὑστερήσαντος οἴνου λέγει ἡ μήτηρ τοῦ Ἰησοῦ πρὸς αὐτόν, And when the wine failed, the mother of Jesus said to him. Jn. 5:13, ὄχλου ὄντος ἐν τῷ τόπῳ.

## D. Dative

**1. Indirect object of a verb.** Jn. 1:25, εἶπαν αὐτῷ, they said to him. Jn. 1:26, ἀπεκρίθη αὐτοῖς.

**2. Possession or personal relationship,** in predicate of εἰμί or γίνομαι. Jn. 13:35, ἐμοὶ μαθηταί ἐστε, you are disciples to me (i.e., my disciples). Mt. 18:12, ἐὰν γένηταί τινι ἀνθρώπῳ ἑκατὸν πρόβατα.

**3. Predicate of various verbs,** and with related adjectives, expressing belief, association, similarity, fitness, etc. Jn. 2:22, ἐπίστευσαν τῇ γραφῇ καὶ τῷ λόγῳ, they believed the Scripture and the word. Jn. 5:10, οὐκ ἔξεστίν σοι, it is not lawful for you. Jn. 9:9, ὅμοιος αὐτῷ ἐστιν.

**4. Instrument or means.** Jn. 11:2, ἦν δὲ Μαριὰμ ἡ ἀλείψασα τὸν κύριον μύρῳ καὶ ἐκμάξασα τοὺς πόδας αὐτοῦ ταῖς θριξὶν αὐτῆς, Now it was Mary who had anointed the Lord with ointment and had wiped his feet with her hair. Jn. 11:44, κειρίαις . . . . σουδαρίῳ.

Occasionally used instead of ὑπό with the genitive to express personal agent. Lk. 23:15, οὐδὲν ἄξιον θανάτου ἐστὶν πεπραγμένον αὐτῷ, nothing worthy of death has been done by him.

5. Cause, reason. Ro. 4:20, οὐ διεκρίθη τῇ ἀπιστίᾳ, he did not hesitate in (i.e., because of) unbelief. Ga. 6:12, ἵνα τῷ σταυρῷ τοῦ Χριστοῦ μὴ διώκωνται, in order that they may not be persecuted because of the cross of Christ. Eph. 2:3, ἤμεθα τέκνα φύσει ὀργῆς.

6. Time when. Jn. 2:1, τῇ ἡμέρᾳ τῇ τρίτῃ, on the third day. Lk. 14:17, τῇ ὥρᾳ τοῦ δείπνου.

7. Reference. The dative names the person or thing to which the statement refers. Jn. 3:26, ᾧ σὺ μεμαρτύρηκας, he with reference to whom you have testified. Mt. 5:3, οἱ πτωχοὶ τῷ πνεύματι.

8. Measure or degree. Jn. 4:41, πολλῷ πλείους ἐπίστευσαν, more people by much (i.e., many more people) believed. Mt. 6:30, πολλῷ μᾶλλον.

9. Manner or mode. Phl. 1:18, παντὶ τρόπῳ, εἴτε προφάσει εἴτε ἀληθείᾳ, Χριστὸς καταγγέλλεται, in every manner, whether in pretence or in truth, Christ is being proclaimed. Ac. 15:1, τῷ ἔθει.

10. Repeats the idea of the verb, for emphasis (cf. the cognate accusative). Jn. 3:29, χαρᾷ χαίρει, he rejoices with joy (i.e., he rejoices greatly). Lk. 22:15, ἐπιθυμίᾳ ἐπεθύμησα.

**E.** Accusative

1. Direct object of verb. Jn. 3:16, ἠγάπησεν ὁ θεὸς τὸν κόσμον, God loved the world. Jn. 3:17, τὸν υἱόν.

2. Subject of an infinitive:

a. Anarthrous infinitive. Jn. 3:14, ὑψωθῆναι δεῖ τὸν υἱὸν τοῦ ἀνθρώπου, it is necessary for the Son of Man to be lifted up. Jn. 21:22, ἐὰν αὐτὸν θέλω μένειν.

b. Articular infinitive. Jn. 2:24, διὰ τὸ αὐτὸν γινώσκειν πάντας, because of his knowing all people. Jn. 1:48, Πρὸ τοῦ σε Φίλιππον φωνῆσαι.

3. Extent of time or space. Jn. 1:39, ἔμειναν τὴν ἡμέραν ἐκείνην, they remained (for the extent of time of) that day. Jn. 6:19, ἐληλακότες οὖν ὡς σταδίους εἴκοσι πέντε ἢ τριάκοντα, Then when they had rowed (to the extent of) about 25 or 30 stadia. Jn. 4:40, δύο ἡμέρας.

4. Cognate accusative. Emphasizes the meaning of the verb by a word in the accusative case related to the verb (cf. Dative 10). Jn. 7:24, τὴν δικαίαν κρίσιν κρίνατε, judge righteous judgment (i.e., judge righteously). Mt. 2:10, ἐχάρησαν χαρὰν μεγάλην.

III. PREPOSITIONS. Gr §118-25,234-307; DM 113; BF §203-40. For prepositions in compound, Gl, Part 2

A. Principal uses and meanings

1. ἀμφί (not used as a separate preposition in the N.T.)

In compound
   Around. Mt. 4:18, βάλλοντας ἀμφιβλήστρον, casting a net-- i.e., an instrument (-τρον) for casting (βλη-, from βάλλω) around (ἀμφι-). Mk. 11:4, ἀμφόδου.

2. ἀνά (general meaning up, opposite of κατά)

With the accusative

a. Throughout. Mk. 7:31, ἀνὰ μέσον τῶν ὁρίων Δεκαπόλεως, throughout the midst of the regions of Decapolis. Mt. 13:25, ἀνὰ μέσον τοῦ σίτου.

b. Apiece (distributive). Jn. 2:6, χωροῦσαι ἀνὰ μετρητὰς δύο ἢ τρεῖς, holding two or three measures apiece. Mt. 20:9, ἔλαβον ἀνὰ δηνάριον.

In compound

a. Up. Jn. 1:51, ἀναβαίνοντας, ascending (going up). Jn. 5:29, ἀνάστασιν.

b. Back again. Lk. 15:24, ἀνέζησεν, he has come to life again. Col. 3:10, τὸν ἀνακαινούμενον.

c. Very much. Lk. 23:18, ἀνέκραγον, they were crying out. Lk. 12:49, ἀνήφθη.

**3.** ἀντί (general meaning *in place of*)

**With the genitive**

**a.** *In place of, instead of.* Mt. 2:22, ἀντὶ τοῦ πατρὸς αὐτοῦ, in place of his father. Lk. 11:11, ἀντὶ ἰχθύος.

**b.** *In exchange for.* Mt. 5:38, ὀφθαλμὸν ἀντὶ ὀφθαλμοῦ, an eye in exchange for an eye. He. 12:16, ἀντὶ βρώσεως μιᾶς.

**c.** *Cause, for.* Eph. 5:31, ἀντὶ τούτου, because of this. He. 12:2, ἀντὶ τῆς προκειμένης αὐτῷ χαρᾶς (alternative meaning, 'instead of').

**d.** *In behalf of, for.* Mt. 17:27, δὸς αὐτοῖς ἀντὶ ἐμοῦ καὶ σοῦ, give it to them in behalf of me and you. Mt. 20:28, ἀντὶ πολλῶν.

**In compound**

**a.** *Opposite to.* Jn. 19:12, πᾶς ὁ βασιλέα ἑαυτὸν ποιῶν ἀντιλέγει τῷ Καίσαρι, Everyone who makes himself a king speaks against Caesar. 1 Jn. 2:18, ἀντίχριστος. Ac. 7:51, ἀντιπίπτετε.

**b.** *On the other side* (from someone, in order to help). Lk. 1:54, ἀντελάβετο Ἰσραὴλ παιδὸς αὐτοῦ, he has helped (taken hold on the other side of) Israel his servant. 1 Cor. 12:28, ἀντιλήμψεις.

**c.** *In return.* Lk. 6:38, ᾧ γὰρ μέτρῳ μετρεῖτε ἀντιμετρηθήσεται ὑμῖν, For with the measure with which you measure it shall be measured to you in return. Lk. 14:12, ἀντικαλέσωσιν.

**4.** ἀπό (general meaning *away from the exterior*, opposite of πρός)

**With the genitive**

**a.** *Away from* (separation). Jn. 10:18, οὐδεὶς αἴρει αὐτὴν ἀπ' ἐμοῦ, No one takes it away from me. Jn. 10:5, ἀπ' αὐτοῦ.

**b.** *From* (source, derivation). Jn. 3:2, οἴδαμεν ὅτι ἀπὸ θεοῦ ἐλήλυθας, we know that you have come from God. Jn. 1:45, ἀπὸ Ναζαρέθ.

**c.** *From* a time past. Jn. 11:53, ἀπ' ἐκείνης οὖν τῆς ἡμέρας, therefore from that day. Lk. 24:27, ἀρξάμενος ἀπὸ Μωϋσέως.

**d.** *Because of.* Lk. 19:3, οὐκ ἠδύνατο ἀπὸ τοῦ ὄχλου, he was not able because of the crowd. Jn. 21:6, ἀπὸ τοῦ πλήθους τῶν ἰχθύων.

## In compound

**a.** *Away from* (separation). Jn. 12:42, ἵνα μὴ ἀποσυνάγωγοι γένωνται, lest they should be put out of the synagogue. Lk. 23:14, ἀποστρέφοντα.

**b.** *Completely* (intensive). Lk. 6:10, ἀπεκατεστάθη ἡ χεὶρ αὐτοῦ, his hand was completely restored. Mk. 13:22, ἀποπλανᾶν.

## 5. διά

### With the genitive

**a.** *Through* (of place). Jn. 4:4, διὰ τῆς Σαμαρείας, through Samaria. Jn. 10:1, διὰ τῆς θύρας.

**b.** *Through* (of time). Mk. 14:58, διὰ τριῶν ἡμέρων, through three days. Lk. 5:5, δι᾽ ὅλης νυκτός.

**c.** *Through* (of agency). Jn. 1:3, δι᾽ αὐτοῦ, through him. Jn. 1:17, διὰ Μωϋσέως.

### With the accusative
*On account of, because of.* Jn. 1:31, διὰ τοῦτο, on account of this. Jn. 3:29, διὰ τὴν φωνήν.

## In compound

**a.** *Through* (of place). Jn. 4:4, διέρχεσθαι, to go through. Lk. 16:26, διαβῆναι.

**b.** *Thoroughly* (intensive). Ac. 8:1, πάντες δὲ διεσπάρησαν, and all were scattered about. Lk. 2:51, διετήρει.

## 6. εἰς (general meaning *into the interior*, opposite of ἐκ)

### With the accusative

**a.** *Into* a place, state, or time. Jn. 1:9, ἐρχόμενον εἰς τὸν κόσμον, coming into the world. Jn. 1:43, εἰς τὴν Γαλιλαίαν. Jn. 6:51, εἰς τὸν αἰῶνα.

**b.** *Regarding, with reference to.* Jn. 8:26, ταῦτα λαλῶ εἰς τὸν κόσμον, these things I speak with regard to the world. Ac. 2:25, λέγει εἰς αὐτόν.

**c.** *Against* (in hostile sense). Jn. 15:21, ταῦτα πάντα ποιήσουσιν εἰς ὑμᾶς, all these things they will do to (i.e., against) you. Ac. 6:11, εἰς Μωϋσῆν.

**d.** *For the purpose of.* Jn. 9:39, εἰς κρίμα, for the purpose of judgment. Jn. 1:7, εἰς μαρτυρίαν.

**e.** *With the result that* (distinct from purpose). He. 11:3, εἰς τὸ μὴ ἐκ φαινομένων τὸ βλεπόμενον γεγονέναι, with the result that that which is seen has not been made from things which appear. Ro. 1:20, εἰς τὸ εἶναι αὐτοὺς ἀναπολογήτους.

**f.** εἰς, prep. phrase, equivalent to predicate of εἰμί or γίνομαι. Jn. 16:20, ἡ λύπη ὑμῶν εἰς χαρὰν γενήσεται, your grief shall become (i.e., be changed into) joy. Mt. 19:5, καὶ ἔσονται οἱ δύο εἰς σάρκα μίαν.

**g.** *In*, having previously gone *into* (with verbs of state). (Cf. the counterpart use of ἐν.) Jn. 1:18, ὁ ὢν εἰς τὸν κόλπον τοῦ πατρός, who has gone into (and is now in) the Father's bosom. Lk. 11:7, τὰ παιδία μου μετ' ἐμοῦ εἰς τὴν κοίτην εἰσίν.

*Note*: The regular Greek expression for "believe in" someone is πιστεύω εἰς with the accusative--i.e., to put one's faith *into* someone. Jn. 2:11, ἐπίστευσαν εἰς αὐτὸν οἱ μαθηταὶ αὐτοῦ, his disciples believed in him.

**In compound**

*Into.* Jn. 10:9, δι' ἐμοῦ ἐάν τις εἰσέλθῃ, If anyone enters through me. Jn. 18:16, εἰσήγαγεν.

**7.** ἐκ (general meaning *from the interior to the exterior*, opposite of εἰς)

**With the genitive**

**a.** *Out of* (movement out of a place). Jn. 2:15, πάντας ἐξέβαλεν ἐκ τοῦ ἱεροῦ, he drove them all out of the temple. Jn. 7:38, ἐκ τῆς κοιλίας αὐτοῦ.

**b.** *From* (source). Jn. 3:27, ἐὰν μὴ ᾖ δεδομένον αὐτῷ ἐκ τοῦ οὐρανοῦ, unless it be given to him from heaven. Jn. 1:13, οὐκ ἐξ αἱμάτων οὐδὲ ἐκ θελήματος σαρκὸς οὐδὲ ἐκ θελήματος ἀνδρὸς ἀλλ' ἐκ θεοῦ.

**c.** *For, from* (of past time). Jn. 9:32, ἐκ τοῦ αἰῶνος οὐκ ἠκούσθη, From eternity it has not been heard. Jn. 9:1, ἐκ γενέτης.

**d.** *From, because of.* Jn. 4:6, κεκοπιακὼς ἐκ τῆς ὁδοιπορίας, wearied from (because of) his journey. Rev. 8:11, ἀπέθανον ἐκ τῶν ὑδάτων.

**e.** *Out of* (material). Jn. 2:15, ποιήσας φραγέλλιον ἐκ σχοινίων, having made a whip out of cords. Jn. 19:2, ἐξ ἀκανθῶν.

**f.** *Of* (partitive). Jn. 1:35, ὁ Ἰωάννης καὶ ἐκ τῶν μαθητῶν αὐτοῦ δύο, John and two (who were a part) of his disciples. Jn. 6:60, πολλοὶ . . . ἐκ τῶν μαθητῶν αὐτοῦ.

**In compound**

**a.** *Forth, out.* Jn. 2:15, πάντας ἐξέβαλεν, he drove them all out. Jn. 15:16, ἐγὼ ἐξελεξάμην ὑμᾶς.

**b.** *Completely* (intensive). Lk. 21:36, δεόμενοι ἵνα κατισχύσητε ἐκφυγεῖν, praying that you may have strength to escape (i.e., to flee completely). Mk. 9:6, ἔκφοβοι.

**8.** ἐν (general meaning *in*)

**With the dative**

**a.** *In* (place or state). Jn. 1:4, ἐν αὐτῷ, in him. Jn. 11:20, ἐν τῷ οἴκῳ.

**b.** *Among.* Jn. 1:14, ἐσκήνωσεν ἐν ἡμῖν, he dwelt among us. Jn. 9:16, ἐν αὐτοῖς.

**c.** *During, while* (of a period of time). Mt. 13:4, ἐν τῷ σπείρειν αὐτόν, while he was sowing. Mk. 1:9, ἐν ἐκείναις ταῖς ἡμέραις, during those days. Jn. 11:9, ἐν τῇ ἡμέρᾳ.

**d.** *At, on, when* (of a specific time). Jn. 5:16, ταῦτα ἐποίει ἐν σαββάτῳ, he was doing these things on a Sabbath. Jn. 6:44, ἐν τῇ ἐσχάτῃ ἡμέρᾳ.

**e.** *With, by* (instrument or means). Mk. 11:28, Ἐν ποίᾳ ἐξουσίᾳ ταῦτα ποιεῖς; By what authority do you do these things? Jn. 13:35, ἐν τούτῳ.

**f.** *In the power of.* Jn. 3:21, ὅτι ἐν θεῷ ἐστιν εἰργασμένα, that they have been wrought in the power of God. Jn. 5:43, ἐν τῷ ὀνόματι.

**g.** *Invested with.* 1 Tim. 1:18, ἵνα στρατεύῃ ἐν αὐταῖς, in order that you may fight invested with them. He. 9:25, ἐν αἵματι ἀλλοτρίῳ.

**h.** *Consisting of.* Eph. 5:9, ὁ γὰρ καρπὸς τοῦ φωτὸς ἐν πάσῃ ἀγαθωσύνῃ, for the fruit of the light consists of all goodness. Eph. 2:15, ἐν δόγμασιν.

**i.** ἐν--prepositional phrase as the equivalent of an adverb of manner. Jn. 7:4, ἐν κρυπτῷ . . . ἐν παρρησίᾳ, in secret . . . in the open (i.e., secretly . . . openly). Lk. 18:8, ἐν τάχει.

**j.** *Into,* resulting in being *in* (with verbs of motion). (Cf. the counterpart use of εἰς.) Lk. 4:1, ἤγετο ἐν τῷ πνεύματι ἐν τῇ ἐρήμῳ, he was led by the Spirit (into and was now) in the wilderness. Jn. 3:35, δέδωκεν ἐν τῇ χειρὶ αὐτοῦ.

## In compound

**a.** *In, into, at.* Mt. 26:67, ἐνέπτυσαν εἰς τὸ πρόσωπον αὐτοῦ, they spat in his face. Jn. 6:17, ἐμβάντες εἰς πλοῖον.

**b.** *Very much* (intensive). Lk. 6:18, οἱ ἐνοχλούμενοι ἀπὸ πνευμάτων ἀκαθάρτων, they who were troubled by unclean spirits. Lk. 24:37, ἔμφοβοι γενόμενοι.

**9.** ἐπί (general meaning *upon*)

## With the genitive

**a.** *At, upon* (place). Jn. 6:19, περιπατοῦντα ἐπὶ τῆς θαλάσσης, walking upon the lake. Mt. 6:10, ἐπὶ γῆς.

**b.** *Over* (of authority). Ac. 8:27, ὃς ἦν ἐπὶ πάσης τῆς γάζης αὐτῆς, who was over all her treasure. Lk. 12:42, ἐπὶ τῆς θεραπείας αὐτοῦ.

**c.** *At the time of.* Ac. 11:28, ἥτις ἐγένετο ἐπὶ Κλαυδίου. Mk. 2:26, ἐπὶ Ἀβιαθὰρ ἀρχιερέως.

## With the dative

**a.** *On, at, near* (place). Jn. 11:38, λίθος ἐπέκειτο ἐπ' αὐτῷ, a stone had been placed upon it. Jn. 4:6, ἐπὶ τῇ πηγῇ.

**b.** *In addition to.* Col. 3:14, ἐπὶ πᾶσιν δὲ τούτοις, and in addition to all these things. Lk. 3:20, ἐπὶ πᾶσιν.

**c.** *On the basis of, at.* Lk. 5:5, ἐπὶ δὲ τῷ ῥήματί σου, on the basis of your word. Lk. 15:7, ἐπὶ ἑνὶ ἁμαρτωλῷ μετανοοῦντι.

**d.** *At the time of, during.* Phl. 1:3, ἐπὶ πάσῃ τῇ μνείᾳ ὑμῶν, at every remembrance of you. Jn. 4:27, ἐπὶ τούτῳ.

## With the accusative

**a.** *To, toward, upon* (place). Jn. 1:32, ἔμεινεν ἐπ' αὐτόν, it remained upon him. Jn. 6:16, ἐπὶ τὴν θάλασσαν.

**b.** *Against* (in hostile sense). Mt. 10:21, ἐπαναστήσονται τέκνα ἐπὶ γονεῖς, children shall rise up against parents. Jn. 13:18, ἐπ' ἐμέ.

**c.** *Over* (authority, superiority). Lk. 1:33, βασιλεύσει ἐπὶ τὸν οἶκον 'Ιακώβ, he shall rule over the house of Jacob. Lk. 2:8, ἐπὶ τὴν ποίμνην αὐτῶν.

**d.** *For, during, at* (time). Lk. 18:4, οὐκ ἤθελεν ἐπὶ χρόνον, he did not want to for a time. Ac. 3:1, ἐπὶ τὴν ὥραν τῆς προσευχῆς.

## In compound

**a.** *Upon* (something, someone). Jn. 3:12, τὰ ἐπίγεια, the earthly (upon earth) things. Jn. 7:30, ἐπέβαλεν.

**b.** *At, to, upon.* Lk. 9:38, ἐπιβλέψαι, to look upon. Lk. 4:17, ἐπεδόθη αὐτῷ.

**c.** *Up.* Ac. 21:4, μὴ ἐπιβαίνειν εἰς 'Ιεροσόλυμα, not to go up into Jerusalem. Jn. 4:35, ἐπάρατε τοὺς ὀφθαλμοὺς ὑμῶν.

**d.** *Completely* (intensive). Lk. 1:4, ἵνα ἐπιγνῷς, in order that you may know thoroughly. Phl. 3:13, τὰ μὲν ὀπίσω ἐπιλανθανόμενος.

**10.** κατά (general meaning *down*, opposite of ἀνά)

## With the genitive

**a.** *Against* (in hostile sense). Lk. 11:23, 'Ο μὴ ὢν μετ' ἐμοῦ κατ' ἐμοῦ ἐστιν, He who is not with me is against me. Jn. 19:11, κατ' ἐμοῦ.

**b.** *By* (in oaths). He. 6:13, ὤμοσεν καθ' ἑαυτοῦ, he took oath by himself. Mt. 26:63, κατὰ τοῦ θεοῦ.

**c.** *Down*. Lk. 8:33, ὥρμησεν ἡ ἀγέλη κατὰ τοῦ κρημνοῦ, the herd rushed down the slope.

**d.** *Throughout*. Lk. 23:5, καθ' ὅλης τῆς Ἰουδαίας, throughout all Judea. Lk. 4:14, καθ' ὅλης τῆς περιχώρου.

### With the accusative

**a.** *In, during* (of time). Mt. 1:20, ἄγγελος κυρίου κατ' ὄναρ ἐφάνη αὐτῷ, an angel of the Lord appeared to him in a dream. Mt. 27:15, Κατὰ δὲ ἑορτήν.

**b.** *By* (distributively). Lk. 22:53, καθ' ἡμέραν, day by day. Mt. 14:13, κατ' ἰδίαν, by himself, alone. Mt. 24:7, κατὰ τόπους.

**c.** *In accordance with, according to*. Jn. 18:31, κατὰ τὸν νόμον ὑμῶν κρίνατε αὐτόν, judge him according to your law. Jn. 2:6, κατὰ τὸν καθαρισμὸν τῶν Ἰουδαίων.

**d.** *In relation to, from the point of view of*. Ro. 1:15, τὸ κατ' ἐμὲ πρόθυμον, the eagerness in relation to me (i.e., my eagerness). Ro. 11:21, τῶν κατὰ φύσιν κλάδων.

### In compound

**a.** *Down*. Jn. 1:32, τεθέαμαι τὸ πνεῦμα καταβαῖνον, I beheld the Spirit coming down. Jn. 17:24, καταβολῆς.

**b.** *Against* (in hostile sense). Jn. 18:29, τίνα κατηγορίαν φέρετε τοῦ ἀνθρώπου τούτου; What accusation do you bring against this man? Mk. 14:60, καταμαρτυροῦσιν.

**c.** *Completely* (intensive). Jn. 2:17, Ὁ ζῆλος τοῦ οἴκου σου καταφάγεταί με, The zeal for your house will consume me (eat me completely). 2 Cor. 11:20, εἴ τις ὑμᾶς καταδουλοῖ.

## 11. μετά

### With the genitive

**a.** *With* (of accompaniment). Jn. 3:2, ἐὰν μὴ ᾖ ὁ θεὸς μετ' αὐτοῦ, unless God be with him. Jn. 4:27, μετὰ γυναικός.

**b.** *With* (of quarreling or hostility). 1 Cor. 6:6, ἀδελφὸς μετὰ ἀδελφοῦ κρίνεται, a brother goes to court against a brother. Jn. 3:25, μετὰ Ἰουδαίου.

c. *With* (of an accompanying feeling). Lk. 8:13, μετὰ χαρᾶς δέχονται τὸν λόγον, with joy they receive the word. Mt. 28:8, μετὰ φόβου καὶ χαρᾶς μεγάλης.

### With the accusative

*After* (of time). Jn. 13:7, γνώσῃ δὲ μετὰ ταῦτα, but you will know after these things. Jn. 13:27, μετὰ τὸ ψωμίον.

### In compound

a. Indicating change. Mk. 9:2, μετεμορφώθη, he was transfigured (i.e., his form was changed). Jn. 5:24, μεταβέβηκεν.

b. *With* (of sharing with someone). Ac. 2:46, μετελάμβανον τροφῆς, they were partaking of food (with one another). 1 Cor. 9:10, μετέχειν.

12. παρά (general meaning *alongside of*)

### With the genitive

*From beside, from.* Jn. 1:6, Ἐγένετο ἄνθρωπος, ἀπεσταλμένος παρὰ θεοῦ, there came a man, sent from God. Jn. 4:9, παρ' ἐμοῦ.

### With the dative

*Beside, with* (generally, at rest). Jn. 1:39, παρ' αὐτῷ ἔμειναν, they remained with him. Jn. 17:5, παρὰ σεαυτῷ . . . παρὰ σοί.

### With the accusative

a. *Alongside of, at* (generally involving motion). Mt. 15:29, ὁ Ἰησοῦς ἦλθεν παρὰ τὴν θάλασσαν τῆς Γαλιλαίας, Jesus passed along the sea of Galilee. Mt. 15:30, παρὰ τοὺς πόδας αὐτοῦ.

b. *Beyond, above, more than.* Lk. 3:13, Μηδὲν πλέον παρὰ τὸ διατεταγμένον ὑμῖν πράσσετε, Exact nothing above what is commanded you. Lk. 13:2, παρὰ πάντας τοὺς Γαλιλαίους.

c. *Contrary to.* Ro. 11:24, παρὰ φύσιν, contrary to nature. Ro. 16:17, παρὰ τὴν διδαχήν.

### In compound

a. *Aside, amiss, contrary to.* Ro. 2:23, διὰ τῆς παραβάσεως τοῦ νόμου, through the transgression of (i.e., going aside from) the law. Ac. 23:3, παρανομῶν.

**b.** *Beyond, away.* Mt. 26:39, παρελθάτω ἀπ' ἐμοῦ τὸ ποτήριον τοῦτο, may this cup pass away from me. Lk. 21:33, παρελεύσονται.

**c.** *Alongside of, by.* Mk. 6:48, ἤθελεν παρελθεῖν αὐτούς, he wanted to come alongside of them. Jn. 18:22, εἷς παρεστηκὼς τῶν ὑπηρετῶν.

**d.** *Strong, strongly* (intensive). He. 3:8, ἐν τῷ παραπικρασμῷ, in the time of strong provocation. Lk. 24:29, καὶ παρεβιάσαντο αὐτόν.

## 13. περί (general meaning, *about*)

### With the genitive

*About, concerning.* Jn. 15:26, ἐκεῖνος μαρτυρήσει περὶ ἐμοῦ, that one will testify concerning me. Jn. 16:8, περὶ ἁμαρτίας καὶ περὶ δικαιοσύνης καὶ περὶ κρίσεως.

### With the accusative

**a.** *Around, about* (of place). Mt. 18:6, περὶ τὸν τράχηλον αὐτοῦ, around his neck. Mt. 8:18, περὶ αὐτόν.

**b.** *Around, about* (of time). Mt. 20:3, περὶ τρίτην ὥραν, about the third hour. Mk. 6:48, περὶ τετάρτην φυλακὴν τῆς νυκτός.

**c.** *With regard to.* 1 Tim. 1:19, περὶ τὴν πίστιν ἐναυάγησαν, with regard to the faith they have made shipwreck. 2 Tim. 3:8, ἀδόκιμοι περὶ τὴν πίστιν.

### In compound

**a.** *Around.* Jn. 11:42, διὰ τὸν ὄχλον τὸν περιεστῶτα, on account of the crowd which is standing around. Jn. 19:2, περιέβαλον.

**b.** *Very much* (intensive). Lk. 18:23, περίλυπος ἐγενήθη, he became very grieved. 1 Th. 4:15, οἱ περιλειπόμενοι.

## 14. πρό (general meaning, *before*)

### With the genitive

**a.** *Before* (of time). Jn. 1:48, Πρὸ τοῦ σε Φίλιππον φωνῆσαι, Before Philip called you. Jn. 11:55, πρὸ τοῦ πάσχα.

**b.** *Before, in front of* (of place). Ac. 12:6, φυλακές τε πρὸ τῆς θύρας, and guards in front of the door. Ac. 12:14, πρὸ τοῦ πυλῶνος.

**c.** *Before, above* (of preference or superiority). Ja. 5:12, πρὸ πάντων, above (more important than) all things. 1 Pe. 4:8, πρὸ πάντων.

**In compound**

**a.** *Before, forth* (of place). Mt. 26:32, προάξω ὑμᾶς, I will go before you. Mk. 14:68, εἰς τὸ προαύλιον.

**b.** *Beforehand* (of time). Mk. 13:11, μὴ προμεριμνᾶτε, do not be anxious beforehand. Mk. 14:8, προέλαβεν.

**15.** πρός (general meaning *to*, opposite of ἀπό)

**With the genitive** (once only in N.T.)
*Advantageous for*. Ac. 27:34, τοῦτο γὰρ πρὸς τῆς ὑμετέρας σωτηρίας ὑπάρχει, for this is advantageous for your health.

**With the dative**
*At*. Jn. 20:11, Μαρία δὲ εἱστήκει πρὸς τῷ μνημείῳ, but Mary stood at the tomb. Jn. 20:12, ἕνα πρὸς τῇ κεφαλῇ καὶ ἕνα πρὸς τοῖς ποσίν.

**With the accusative**

**a.** *To* (implying arrival). Jn. 1:19, ἀπέστειλαν πρὸς αὐτόν, they sent to him. Jn. 1:42, πρὸς τὸν Ἰησοῦν.

**b.** *Toward, in the direction of* (not having arrived). Jn. 1:29, ἐρχόμενον πρὸς αὐτόν, coming toward him. Jn. 1:47, πρὸς αὐτόν.

**c.** *Toward* (a time), *for* (a period of time). Lk. 24:29, πρὸς ἑσπέραν ἐστίν, it is toward evening. Jn. 5:35, πρὸς ὥραν.

**d.** *To* (equivalent of indirect object). Jn. 2:3, λέγει ἡ μήτηρ τοῦ Ἰησοῦ πρὸς αὐτόν, the mother of Jesus said to him. Jn. 6:28, εἶπον οὖν πρὸς αὐτόν.

**e.** *At, with, in the presence of*. Jn. 1:1, ὁ λόγος ἦν πρὸς τὸν θεόν, the Word was in the presence of God. Jn. 11:32, πρὸς τοὺς πόδας.

**f.** *Against* (in hostile sense). 1 Cor. 6:1, πρᾶγμα ἔχων πρὸς τὸν ἕτερον, having a matter against another person. Jn. 6:52, Ἐμάχοντο οὖν πρὸς ἀλλήλους.

**g.** *Pertaining to.* Jn. 13:28, οὐδεὶς ἔγνω . . . πρὸς τί εἶπεν αὐτῷ, no one knew why (i.e., pertaining to what) he said it to him. He. 1:7, πρὸς μὲν τοὺς ἀγγέλους, with reference to the angels. Jn. 21:22, τί πρὸς σέ;

**h.** *For the purpose of.* Ro. 3:26, πρὸς τὴν ἔνδειξιν τῆς δικαιοσύνης αὐτοῦ, for the purpose of showing his righteousness. Mt. 6:1, πρὸς τὸ θεαθῆναι αὐτοῖς.

**i.** *Resulting in.* Jn. 11:4, Αὕτη ἡ ἀσθένεια οὐκ ἔστιν πρὸς θάνατον, This sickness is not to (i.e., will not result in) death. 1 Jn. 5:16, πρὸς θάνατον (2 examples).

### In compound

**a.** *To.* Jn. 12:21, οὗτοι οὖν προσῆλθον Φιλίππῳ, these men came to Philip. Jn. 16:2, προσφέρειν.

**b.** *Toward, in the direction of.* Ac. 27:27, προσάγειν τινὰ αὐτοῖς χώραν, some land to be coming near to them.

**c.** *In addition.* Lk. 3:20, προσέθηκεν καὶ τοῦτο, he added this also. Lk. 19:16, προσηργάσατο.

**16.** σύν (general meaning *with*)

### With the dative
*Together with.* Jn. 12:2, εἷς ἦν ἐκ τῶν ἀνακειμένων σὺν αὐτῷ, he was one of those who were at table with him. Jn. 21:3, σὺν σοί.

### In compound
*Together, fellow-, co-* (with). Jn. 11:16, τοῖς συμμαθηταῖς, to the fellow-disciples. Jn. 4:36, συνάγει.

**17.** ὑπέρ (general meaning *over*, opposite of ὑπό)

### With the genitive

**a.** *In behalf of, for the sake of.* Jn. 17:19, ὑπὲρ αὐτῶν, for their sake. Jn. 11:4, ὑπὲρ τῆς δόξης τοῦ θεοῦ.

**b.** *Concerning, in reference to.* Ro. 9:27, κράζει ὑπὲρ τοῦ Ἰσραήλ, he cries concerning Israel. Jn. 1:30, ὑπὲρ οὗ.

### With the accusative

**a.** *Above, beyond* (of superiority). Mt. 10:24, Οὐκ ἔστιν μαθητὴς ὑπὲρ τὸν διδάσκαλον, A disciple is not above his teacher. Eph. 1:22, ὑπὲρ πάντα.

**b.** *Above, more than* (of excess). Mt. 10:37, ὁ φιλῶν πατέρα ἢ μητέρα ὑπὲρ ἐμέ, He who loves father or mother more than me. Ac. 26:13, ὑπὲρ τὴν λαμπρότητα τοῦ ἡλίου.

### In compound

**a.** *Above, beyond* (of place). 2 Cor. 10:16, εἰς τὰ ὑπερέκεινα, into the regions beyond you. Ac. 1:13, εἰς τὸ ὑπερῷον.

**b.** *Over* (of authority or excellence). Phl. 3:8, διὰ τὸ ὑπερέχον τῆς γνώσεως Χριστοῦ, because of the excellence of the knowledge of Christ. Ro. 13:1, ἐξουσίαις ὑπερεχούσαις.

**c.** *Above what is proper.* 1 Th. 4:6, τὸ μὴ ὑπερβαίνειν, not to go beyond what is proper. 1 Pe. 5:5, Ὁ θεὸς ὑπερηφάνοις ἀντιτάσσεται.

**d.** *Over* (implying neglect or non-action). Ac. 17:30, τοὺς . . . χρόνους τῆς ἀγνοίας ὑπεριδών, having overlooked the times of ignorance.

**e.** *Greatly, very much* (intensive use). 2 Th. 1:3, ὑπεραυξάνει ἡ πίστις ὑμῶν, your faith grows exceedingly. Ro. 8:37, ὑπερνικῶμεν.

**18.** ὑπό (general meaning *under*, opposite of ὑπέρ)

### With the genitive

*By* (agency). Lk. 21:24, Ἰερουσαλὴμ ἔσται πατουμένη ὑπὸ ἐθνῶν, Jerusalem shall be trodden down by Gentiles. Jn. 14:21, ὑπὸ τοῦ πατρός μου.

### With the accusative

**a.** *Under* (of place). Jn. 1:48, ὑπὸ τὴν συκῆν, under the fig tree. Mt. 5:15, ὑπὸ τὸν μόδιον.

**b.** *Under* (of authority or power). Mt. 8:9, ἔχων ὑπ᾽ ἐμαυτὸν στρατιώτας, having soldiers under me. Ro. 6:14, οὐ γάρ ἐστε ὑπὸ νόμον ἀλλὰ ὑπὸ χάριν.

## In compound

**a.** *Under* (of place). Mt. 5:35, ὑποπόδιόν ἐστιν τῶν ποδῶν αὐτοῦ, it is the footstool (under-foot-thing) of his feet. Jn. 1:27, τοῦ ὑποδήματος.

**b.** *Behind, back* (of place). Lk. 2:43, ὑπέμεινεν 'Ιησοῦς, Jesus remained behind. Lk. 2:45, ὑπέστρεψαν εἰς 'Ιερουσαλήμ.

**c.** *Under* (of subjection). Mt. 8:27, καὶ οἱ ἄνεμοι καὶ ἡ θάλασσα αὐτῷ ὑπακούουσιν, even the winds and the sea obey him (i.e., are *subject* to what they *hear*). Lk. 10:17, τὰ δαιμόνια ὑποτάσσεται ἡμῖν.

**d.** *Under* (as a pattern to be followed). Lk. 6:47, ὑποδείξω ὑμῖν τίνι ἐστὶν ὅμοιος, I will show you whom he is like. Jn. 13:15, ὑπόδειγμα γὰρ ἔδωκα ὑμῖν.

**e.** *Under* (of hospitality, under one's roof). Lk. 10:38, Μάρθα ὑπεδέξατο αὐτόν, Martha received him (into her house). Ac. 17:7, οὓς ὑποδέδεκται 'Ιάσων.

**f.** *Under* (to submit for consideration). Ac. 13:25, Τί ἐμὲ ὑπονοεῖτε εἶναι; What do you suppose (i.e., submit to your mind for consideration) me to be? Jn. 14:26, ὑπομνήσει ὑμᾶς πάντα.

**g.** *Not much, gently* (intensive use, opposite of ὑπέρ). Ac. 27:13, 'Υποπνεύσαντος δὲ νότου, When the wind blew gently.

## B. Exceptions to the basic rules of usage

**1.** The intensive use of a compounded preposition sometimes loses its intensive force.

**a.** It may become *synonymous with* the uncompounded form. Cf. ἐρωτάω and ἐπερωτάω--Mt. 16:13, ἠρώτα τοὺς μαθητὰς αὐτοῦ, he asked his disciples; Mk. 8:27, ἐπηρώτα τοὺς μαθητὰς αὐτοῦ.

**b.** It may be used *instead of* the uncompounded form; e.g., ὄλλυμι, 'destroy', does not occur in the N.T., but ἀπόλλυμι is common.

**2.** A prepositional phrase sometimes has the same meaning as a case without a preposition.
Cf. Lk. 19:29, δύο τῶν μαθητῶν, two of the disciples; Jn. 1:35, ἐκ τῶν μαθητῶν αὐτοῦ δύο.

Cf. Jn. 6:44, κἀγὼ ἀναστήσω αὐτὸν ἐν τῇ ἐσχάτῃ ἡμέρᾳ, and I will raise him up on the last day; Jn. 6:54, κἀγὼ ἀναστήσω αὐτὸν τῇ ἐσχάτῃ ἡμέρᾳ.

Cf. Jn. 2:3, λέγει ἡ μήτηρ τοῦ 'Ιησοῦ πρὸς αὐτόν, the mother of Jesus said to him; Jn. 2:4, λέγει αὐτῇ ὁ 'Ιησοῦς.

3. Some prepositions are at times apparently interchanged with others with little or no difference in meaning. Each passage must, however, be studied individually in such cases to determine whether a difference in meaning is intended. Gr §308-14

Cf. Mt. 7:16, ἀπὸ τῶν καρπῶν αὐτῶν ἐπιγνώσεσθε αὐτούς, from their fruits you will recognize them; Lk. 6:44, ἐκ τοῦ ἰδίου καρποῦ.

Cf. Ro. 3:26, πρὸς τὴν ἔνδειξιν τῆς δικαιοσύνης αὐτοῦ, for the purpose of demonstrating his righteousness; Ro. 3:26, εἰς τὸ εἶναι αὐτὸν δίκαιον.

Cf. Jn. 10:32, διὰ ποῖον αὐτῶν ἔργον, because of which work of them? Jn. 10:33, περὶ καλοῦ ἔργου . . . περὶ βλασφημίας.

C. Some adverbs, especially adverbs of place, may be used as prepositions; most of them take the genitive case. Gr §133,400

E.g., Mk. 8:23, ἔξω τῆς κώμης, outside the village; Lk. 4:39, ἐπάνω αὐτῆς, over her.

D. If a preposition is repeated before each of a series of nouns, each is given separate prominence; if the preposition is not repeated, they are to be considered as a unit (cf. Granville Sharp's rule for the definite article, I.B.11. above).

E.g., Mt. 22:37, ἐν ὅλῃ τῇ καρδίᾳ σου καὶ ἐν ὅλῃ τῇ ψυχῇ σου καὶ ἐν ὅλῃ τῇ διανοίᾳ σου, with all your heart and with all your soul and with all your mind (the repetition adding emphasis); but cf. 2 Th. 2:9, ἐν πάσῃ δυνάμει καὶ σημείοις καὶ τέρασιν ψεύδους, with all power and signs and false wonders (considered as a whole).

E. A verb compounded with a preposition may take its predicate in one of the following forms (Gr §314, note):

1. The case required by the simple verb. Mt. 21:41, οἵτινες ἀποδώσουσιν αὐτῷ τοὺς καρπούς, who will render to him the fruits.

2. A prepositional phrase using the same or a similar preposition as that which is compounded, the prepositional phrase taking its normal case. Jn. 9:15, πηλὸν ἐπέθηκέν μου ἐπὶ τοὺς ὀφθαλμούς, he placed clay upon my eyes.

3. The case required by the compounded preposition, but without repeating the preposition. Mt. 13:1, ἐξελθὼν ὁ ᾿Ιησοῦς τῆς οἰκίας, Jesus having gone out of the house. Jn. 19:32, τοῦ ἄλλου τοῦ συσταυρωθέντος αὐτῷ, of the other one who was crucified with him.

**IV. ADJECTIVES. Gr §315-31**

A. Greek sometimes uses an adjective where English requires an adverb. Ac. 12:10, ἥτις αὐτομάτη ἠνοίγη αὐτοῖς, which opened to them automatically.

B. Constructions forming comparisons

1. Genitive of comparison
   The second member of the comparison is placed in the genitive case. Jn. 8:53, μὴ σὺ μείζων εἶ τοῦ πατρὸς ἡμῶν ᾿Αβραάμ; Are *you* greater than our *father* Abraham? Jn. 5:36, ᾿Εγὼ δὲ ἔχω τὴν μαρτυρίαν μείζω τοῦ ᾿Ιωάννου.

2. The second member of the comparison may be placed in the same case as that of the first member, joined by ἤ, 'than'. Jn. 4:1, ᾿Ιησοῦς πλείονας μαθητὰς ποιεῖ καὶ βαπτίζει ἢ ᾿Ιωάννης, *Jesus* was making and baptizing more disciples than *John.* Jn. 3:19, ἠγάπησαν οἱ ἄνθρωποι μᾶλλον τὸ σκότος ἢ τὸ φῶς.

3. The second member of the comparison is sometimes placed in a prepositional phrase, ὑπέρ with the accusative or παρά with the accusative. Lk. 16:8, οἱ υἱοὶ τοῦ αἰῶνος τούτου φρονιμώτεροι ὑπὲρ τοὺς υἱοὺς τοῦ φωτός, the sons of this age are wiser *than* the sons of light. He. 11:4, πλείονα θυσίαν ῎Αβελ παρὰ Κάϊν προσήνεγκεν.

C. The comparative degree of the adjective is sometimes used for the superlative. 1 Cor. 13:13, μείζων δὲ τούτων ἡ ἀγάπη, but the *greatest* of these (three) is love. Mt. 18:1, τίς ἄρα μείζων ἐστὶν ἐν τῇ βασιλείᾳ τῶν οὐρανῶν;

## V. PRONOUNS. Gr §332-52

Some exceptions to normal syntax of relative pronouns.
BF §294-6

A. When the antecedent of a relative pronoun is a pronoun or some other easily understood word such as "person," "time," etc., the antecedent is ordinarily omitted. Jn. 18:26, συγγενὴς ὢν οὗ ἀπέκοψεν Πέτρος τὸ ὠτίον, being a kinsman *of him whose* ear Peter cut off (not "a kinsman whose ear . . ."). Jn. 5:21, ὁ υἱὸς οὓς θέλει ζῳοποιεῖ.

B. The relative pronoun may be attracted to the *case* of its antecedent. Jn. 4:14, ἐκ τοῦ ὕδατος οὗ (for ὃ) ἐγὼ δώσω αὐτῷ, from the water which (*not* of which) I will give him. Jn. 17:12, ἐν τῷ ὀνόματί σου ᾧ (for ὃ) δέδωκάς μοι.

   1. If the omission of the antecedent leaves a dangling preposition or other incomplete construction, the relative pronoun *must* take the place and case of the antecedent. Jn. 7:31, μὴ πλείονα σημεῖα ποιήσει ὧν (for τῶν σημείων ἃ) οὗτος ἐποίησεν; will he do more miracles than (the miracles) which this man has done? Jn. 17:9, ἐγὼ ἐρωτῶ . . . περὶ ὧν (for περὶ τῶν ἀνθρώπων οὓς) δέδωκάς μοι, I ask concerning the people whom you have given me. He. 5:8, ἔμαθεν ἀφ' ὧν ἔπαθεν τὴν ὑπακοήν.

   2. The relative pronoun sometimes replaces, and takes the case of, the article of its antecedent. Jn. 11:6, ἔμεινεν ἐν ᾧ ἦν τόπῳ (i.e., ἐν τῷ τόπῳ ἐν ᾧ ἦν), he remained in the place in which he was. Jn. 9:14, ἐν ᾗ ἡμέρᾳ.

C. Occasionally, the *antecedent* is attracted to the case of the relative pronoun (the opposite of B. above). 1 Cor. 10:16, τὸν ἄρτον (for ὁ ἄρτος) ὃν κλῶμεν, οὐχὶ κοινωνία τοῦ σώματος τοῦ Χριστοῦ ἐστιν; Is not the bread which we break a sharing in the body of Christ? Mk. 6:16, ὃν ἐγὼ ἀπεκεφάλισα Ἰωάννην (for Ἰωάννης), οὗτος ἠγέρθη, he whom I beheaded, John, this one has been raised.

D. The relative pronoun sometimes takes the gender of its *predicate* instead of that of its antecedent, when the predicate is an explanation of or a more precise identification of the antecedent. Mk. 15:16, ἔσω τῆς αὐλῆς, ὅ (for ἥ) ἐστιν πραιτώριον, inside the hall, which is the praetorium. Ga. 3:16, Καὶ τῷ σπέρματί σου, ὅς (for ὅ) ἐστιν Χριστός.

**E.** The neuter relative pronoun is sometimes used as an adverb.

**1.** ὅ, 'whereas'. Ro. 6:10, ὃ γὰρ ἀπέθανεν . . . ὃ δὲ ζῇ, For *whereas* he died . . . and *whereas* he lives. Ga. 2:20, ὃ δὲ νῦν ζῶ.

**2.** οὗ, 'where'. Lk. 4:16, Καὶ ἦλθεν εἰς Ναζαρά, οὗ ἦν τεθραμμένος, And he came into Nazareth, *where* he had been brought up. Lk. 4:17, τὸν τόπον οὗ ἦν γεγραμμένον.

**F.** The pronoun αὐτός is sometimes used redundantly with a relative pronoun. Mk. 7:25, γυνὴ . . . ἧς εἶχεν τὸ θυγάτριον αὐτῆς πνεῦμα ἀκάθαρτον, a woman . . . of whom the daughter of her (i.e., a woman whose daughter) had an unclean spirit. Jn. 1:27, οὗ οὐκ εἰμὶ ἐγὼ ἄξιος ἵνα λύσω αὐτοῦ τὸν ἱμάντα τοῦ ὑποδήματος.

## VI. VERBS. Bu (all); Gr §353-97; DM 155-233

**A.** Uses of voice

**1.** Active--the subject does what the verb expresses; e.g., "The disciples saw."

**2.** Middle--the subject acts upon itself (e.g., "He washed himself") or acts for its own benefit (e.g., "He washed the apple for himself").

**3.** Passive--the object of the verb in the active voice becomes the subject in the passive voice; e.g., "I gave him the book" becomes "The book was given to him by me." Occasionally the indirect object in the active voice becomes the subject in the passive voice; e.g., "He was given the book by me."

**4.** Deponent verbs have no active forms, and their middle or passive forms take active meanings; e.g., ἔρχομαι, I go.

**B.** Uses of moods. Bu 73-81

**1.** Indicative--mood of fact. Jn. 1:14, ὁ λόγος σάρξ ἐγένετο, the Word became flesh. Jn. 1:14, ἐσκήνωσεν.

**2.** Imperative--mood of command. Used in commands, entreaties, prayers, requests, etc., both affirmative and negative (except for the negative form with the aorist tense, which takes the subjunctive mood--see 3.d. below). Jn. 17:11, πάτερ ἅγιε, τήρησον αὐτούς, Holy Father, keep them. Jn. 5:14, μηκέτι ἁμάρτανε, don't be sinning any longer. Jn. 16:24, αἰτεῖτε.

**3.** Subjunctive--mood of contingency:

**a.** Hortatory subjunctive, first person plural. Used in exhortations. Jn. 19:24, μὴ σχίσωμεν αὐτόν, let's not divide it. Jn. 11:16, ἄγωμεν.

**b.** Deliberative questions, real or rhetorical. Deal with what is desirable, possible, necessary, or obligatory. Jn. 6:28, τί ποιῶμεν; What should we do? Jn. 19:15, τὸν βασιλέα ὑμῶν σταυρώσω;

**c.** The aorist subjunctive with the double negative οὐ μή is used as an emphatic future negation. Jn. 6:35, ὁ ἐρχόμενος πρὸς ἐμὲ οὐ μὴ πεινάσῃ, He who comes to me will by no means hunger. Jn. 6:37, οὐ μὴ ἐκβάλω.

**d.** Negative commands in the aorist tense take the subjunctive mood instead of the imperative. Lk. 21:8, μὴ πλανηθῆτε . . . μὴ πορευθῆτε ὀπίσω αὐτῶν, do not be deceived . . . do not go after them. Jn. 3:7, μὴ θαυμάσῃς.

**e.** In various dependent clauses of contingency. Jn. 1:8, ἵνα μαρτυρήσῃ, in order that he might testify. Jn. 3:12, ἐὰν εἴπω ὑμῖν, if I should tell you. Jn. 15:7, ὃ ἐὰν θέλητε.

**4.** Optative--mood of wish or hope (rare in N.T.).

**a.** To express a wish, prayer, or imprecation. 1 Th. 5:23, Αὐτὸς δὲ ὁ θεὸς τῆς εἰρήνης ἁγιάσαι ὑμᾶς ὁλοτελεῖς, May the God of peace himself make you completely holy. Ac. 8:20, Τὸ ἀργύριόν σου σὺν σοὶ εἴη εἰς ἀπώλειαν, May your money be with you in perdition! 1 Pe. 5:10, ῾Ο δὲ θεὸς . . . αὐτὸς καταρτίσει, στηρίξει, σθενώσει, θεμελιώσει.

**b.** In indirect questions, implying doubt or hesitancy (Luke-Acts only). Ac. 10:17, διηπόρει ὁ Πέτρος τί ἂν εἴη τὸ ὅραμα, Peter was perplexed as to what the vision might be. Lk. 1:29, διελογίζετο ποταπὸς εἴη ὁ ἀσπασμὸς οὗτος.

**c.** In direct questions, implying doubt or perplexity (3 examples only in N.T.). Ac. 8:31, Πῶς γὰρ ἂν δυναίμην . . . ; For how might I be able . . . ? Ac. 17:18, Τί ἂν θέλοι ὁ σπερμολόγος οὗτος λέγειν;

**d.** In conditional clauses of fact or contingency, with εἰ, implying doubt or hesitancy. Ac. 24:19, εἴ τι ἔχοιεν πρὸς ἐμέ, if perchance they have something against me. 1 Pe. 3:14, εἰ καὶ πάσχοιτε διὰ δικαιοσύνην.

**C.** Tense-aspects of the indicative mood. Bu 6-45; Gr §360-70

Outline of tenses of the indicative mood. Gr §65

| | Present time | Past time | Future time |
|---|---|---|---|
| Continued action | γράφω<br>Present tense<br>'I am writing' | ἔγραφον<br>Imperfect tense<br>'I was writing' | γράψω<br>Future tense<br>'I shall be writing' |
| Undefined or simple action | γράφω<br>Present tense<br>'I write' | ἔγραψα<br>Aorist tense<br>'I wrote' | γράψω<br>Future tense<br>'I shall write' |
| Perfective action (with resulting state) | γέγραφα<br>Perfect tense<br>'I am in a condition resulting from having written' | ἐγεγράμην<br>Pluperfect tense<br>'I was in a condition resulting from having written previously' | ἔσομαι γεγραφώς<br>Future perfect tense<br>'I shall be in a condition resulting from having written (prior to that condition)' |

1. Present

a. Present action in progress or repeated. Jn. 1:48, πόθεν με γινώσκεις; From where do you know me? Jn. 1:50, πιστεύεις;
   *Note:* Except where otherwise indicated, these uses include verbs of state as well as verbs of action.

b. Simple event in present time. Jn. 3:3, ᾿Αμὴν ἀμὴν λέγω σοι, Truly, truly, I say to you. Jn. 4:9, αἰτεῖς.

c. Gnomic present: customary action or general truth. Jn. 2:10, πᾶς ἄνθρωπος πρῶτον τὸν καλὸν οἶνον τίθησιν, Every man (customarily) sets out the good wine first. Jn. 3:8, τὸ πνεῦμα . . . πνεῖ.

d. Conative present: tendency or attempt in present time. Ga. 5:4, οἵτινες ἐν νόμῳ δικαιοῦσθε, you who are attempting to be justified by law. Jn. 10:32, λιθάζετε.

e. Historic present: present tense used to relate a past event. Jn. 1:29, Τῇ ἐπαύριον βλέπει τὸν ᾿Ιησοῦν, On the next day he saw Jesus. Jn. 1:29, λέγει.

f. Futuristic present: the present tense used for the future. Jn. 14:2, πορεύομαι ἑτοιμάσαι τόπον ὑμῖν, I am going (to go) to prepare a place for you. Jn. 14:3, πάλιν ἔρχομαι, I shall come again. Jn. 14:19, ὁ κόσμος με οὐκέτι θεωρεῖ.

**g.** Past action continuing into the present (requires a specific phrase expressing the past aspect). Lk. 15:29, τοσαῦτα ἔτη δουλεύω σοι, for so many years (in the past) I have been serving you (and I still am). Jn. 14:9, Τοσούτῳ χρόνῳ μεθ' ὑμῶν εἰμι.

## 2. Imperfect

**a.** Action in progress (or state existing) in past time. Jn. 2:25, αὐτὸς γὰρ ἐγίνωσκεν τί ἦν ἐν τῷ ἀνθρώπῳ, for he himself knew (continually) what was in man. Jn. 11:36, ἐφίλει.

**b.** Action repeated in past time. Jn. 5:18, οὐ μόνον ἔλυεν τὸ σάββατον, ἀλλὰ καὶ πατέρα ἴδιον ἔλεγεν τὸν θεόν, he was not only (repeatedly) breaking the Sabbath, but was also (more than once) calling God his own father. Jn. 2:23, τὰ σημεῖα ἃ ἐποίει.

**c.** Customary (regularly repeated) action in past time. Ac. 3:2, ὃν ἐτίθουν καθ' ἡμέραν, whom they were accustomed to place daily. Mk. 15:6, ἀπέλυεν.

**d.** *Action* begun in past time. (Cf. the aorist of the beginning of a *state*.) Lk. 5:6, διερρήσσετο δὲ τὰ δίκτυα αὐτῶν, and their nets were beginning to break. Jn. 13:22, ἔβλεπον εἰς ἀλλήλους οἱ μαθηταί.

**e.** Intention, or action attempted but not carried out, in past time. Mk. 15:23, καὶ ἐδίδουν αὐτῷ ἐσμυρνισμένον οἶνον, ὃς δὲ οὐκ ἔλαβεν, and they attempted to give him wine mixed with myrrh, but he did not take it. Ac. 7:26, συνήλλασσεν αὐτούς.

**f.** Impossible, impractical, or hesitant wish. Ro. 9:3, ηὐχόμην γὰρ ἀνάθεμα εἶναι αὐτὸς ἐγὼ ἀπὸ τοῦ Χριστοῦ ὑπὲρ τῶν ἀδελφῶν μου, For I myself could pray to be accursed from Christ for the sake of my brothers (i.e., recognizing the impossibility of God's granting such a wish). Phm. 13, ὃν ἐγὼ ἐβουλόμην πρὸς ἐμαυτὸν κατέχειν, whom I could have desired to keep with myself. Lk. 15:16, ἐπεθύμει γεμίσαι τὴν κοιλίαν αὐτοῦ ἐκ τῶν κερατίων.

## 3. Aorist

**a.** Action completed in past time--considered as a whole or as a single fact. Jn. 1:11, οἱ ἴδιοι αὐτὸν οὐ παρέλαβον, his own people did not receive him. Jn. 1:12, ἔδωκεν.

**b.** Inceptive--the beginning of a *state*. (Cf. the imperfect of the beginning of an *action*.) Ac. 7:60, καὶ τοῦτο εἰπὼν ἐκοιμήθη, And when he had said this he fell asleep. Lk. 15:32, ὁ ἀδελφός σου . . . ἔζησεν.

**c.** Epistolary--in letters, to refer to what will be a past action when the letter is read although it is not past when the letter is being written. Phl. 2:28, ἔπεμψα αὐτόν, I have sent him (with this letter). Ga. 6:11, Ἴδετε πηλίκοις ὑμῖν γράμμασιν ἔγραψα τῇ ἐμῇ χειρί (referring to the letters of this sentence).

**d.** Gnomic--general or proverbial truth (less common than the gnomic present). 1 Pe. 1:24, ἐξηράνθη ὁ χόρτος, καὶ τὸ ἄνθος ἐξέπεσεν, the grass withers and the flower falls off (each year). Jn. 15:6, ἐβλήθη . . . ἐξηράνθη.

## 4. Future

**a.** Undefined or simple action in future time. Jn. 14:26, τὸ πνεῦμα τὸ ἅγιον ὃ πέμψει ὁ πατήρ, the Holy Spirit, whom the Father will send. Jn. 14:3, παραλήμψομαι.

**b.** Action in progress in future time. Jn. 14:30, οὐκέτι πόλλα λαλήσω μεθ᾽ ὑμῶν, No longer shall I be speaking much with you. Jn. 14:12, ποιήσει.

**c.** Declarative future (imperative sense). Mt. 1:21, καλέσεις τὸ ὄνομα αὐτοῦ Ἰησοῦν, you shall (i.e., you must) call his name Jesus. Mt. 19:18-19, οὐ φονεύσεις, οὐ μοιχεύσεις, οὐ κλέψεις, οὐ ψευδομαρτυρήσεις, . . . καὶ ἀγαπήσεις . . .

**d.** The future indicative used for the aorist subjunctive, in various constructions where the subjunctive is normally used. Jn. 6:68 (a deliberative question), κύριε, πρὸς τίνα ἀπελευσόμεθα (for ἀπέλθωμεν); Lord, to whom could we go? Jn. 4:14, οὐ μὴ διψήσει (for διψήσῃ).

## 5. Perfect (present perfect)

Has a double emphasis: present state resulting from past action (is therefore not merely equivalent to the English perfect tense). Jn. 1:34, κἀγὼ ἑώρακα, καὶ μεμαρτύρηκα, and I am in a condition resulting from having seen, and I have borne a testimony whose results continue. Jn. 2:10, τετήρηκας. Jn. 3:13, ἀναβέβηκεν.

**6.** Pluperfect (past perfect)

Has a double emphasis: past state resulting from previous action (is therefore not merely equivalent to the English pluperfect tense). Jn. 1:24 (written periphrastically in this instance), ἀπεσταλμένοι ἦσαν ἐκ τῶν Φαρισαίων, they had been sent (i.e., they were there with John as a result of having been sent) from the Pharisees. Jn. 4:8, οἱ γὰρ μαθηταὶ αὐτοῦ ἀπεληλύθεισαν εἰς τὴν πόλιν, for his disciples were gone (i.e., they had gone and were still away) into the city. Jn. 6:17, ἐγεγόνει.

**7.** Future perfect (rare in the N.T., and occurring only periphrastically)

Has a double emphasis: future state resulting from action prior to that state (not necessarily prior to the statement) (is therefore not merely equivalent to the English future perfect tense). He. 2:13, ἐγὼ ἔσομαι πεποιθὼς ἐπ' αὐτῷ, I shall be in a condition resulting from previously having come to trust in him. Lk. 6:40, κατηρτισμένος δὲ πᾶς ἔσται.

*Note*: In the three perfect tenses, the "resulting state" commonly refers to the subject of the verb, but it may refer to another participant or to the situation in general. Jn. 2:10, σὺ τετήρηκας τὸν καλὸν οἶνον ἕως ἄρτι, you have kept the good wine until now. Jn. 19:22, ἀπεκρίθη ὁ Πιλᾶτος, ''Ο γέγραφα, γέγραφα, Pilate answered, "What I have written, I have written (i.e., it will remain there)!"

**D.** Tense-aspects of other moods (but see also tenses of participles, F.1. below)

**1.** Present. Denotes continuing or repeated action. (The *time* of the action is determined by the leading verb or by the context.) Jn. 1:33, βαπτίζειν ἐν ὕδατι, to baptize (habitually) in water. Jn. 1:43, ἀκολούθει μοι.

**2.** Aorist. Denotes action conceived of as completed (at a time determined by the leading verb or by the context). Jn. 1:7 (action undefined as to its extent), ἵνα μαρτυρήσῃ, in order that he might testify. Jn. 2:7, γεμίσατε.

**3.** Perfect. Denotes a state (at a time determined by the leading verb or by the context) resulting from prior action. Jn. 17:19 (perfect passive subjunctive, written periphrastically), ἵνα ὦσιν . . . ἡγιασμένοι, in order that they may be in a sanctified condition (resulting from prior sanctifying action). Mk. 4:39 (perfect passive imperative), πεφίμωσο, Be in a muzzled condition!

**4.** Future (rare in N.T.). Denotes action at a time future to the leading verb. Ac. 23:30, μηνυθείσης δέ μοι ἐπιβουλῆς εἰς τὸν ἄνδρα ἔσεσθαι, but when a plot was revealed to me which was going to be against the man. Ac. 24:15 (with the future tense further reinforced by μέλλειν, as also in Ac. 11:28 and 27:10), μέλλειν ἔσεσθαι.

**E.** The infinitive: its functions. BF §388-410; Bu 146-63; Gr §385-93
   *Note*: These infinitival functions--purpose, result (rarely), and substantive--may be expressed by various infinitive constructions.

**1.** The anarthrous infinitive (the infinitive without the article)

   **a.** To express purpose. Jn. 4:15, ἵνα μὴ διψῶ μηδὲ διέρχομαι ἐνθάδε ἀντλεῖν, in order that I may not thirst nor come here to draw (i.e., for the purpose of drawing) water. Jn. 1:33, βαπτίζειν.

   **b.** Rarely, to express result distinct from purpose. Rev. 5:5, ἐνίκησεν . . . ἀνοῖξαι τὸ βιβλίον, he has conquered, with the result that he can open the scroll.

   **c.** Used as a substantive: as a noun, or translated as a substantive clause.

   **1)** As a subject, object, in apposition, etc. Jn. 1:43, ἠθέλησεν ἐξελθεῖν, he wished to go out. Jn. 4:4, διέρχεσθαι.

   **2)** To define, limit, or give content of nouns, adjectives, etc. Jn. 1:12, ἔδωκεν αὐτοῖς ἐξουσίαν τέκνα θεοῦ γενέσθαι, he gave them authority to become children of God (i.e., becoming children of God is the content of the authority granted). Jn. 13:10, οὐκ ἔχει χρείαν εἰ μὴ . . . νίψασθαι.

   **3)** To express indirect discourse and other indirect statements. Jn. 4:40, ἠρώτων αὐτὸν μεῖναι παρ᾽ αὐτοῖς, they began asking him to remain with them (i.e., the indirect form of "Remain with us"). Mt. 16:13, Τίνα λέγουσιν οἱ ἄνθρωποι εἶναι τὸν υἱὸν τοῦ ἀνθρώπου; Whom do people say the Son of Man to be (i.e., say that the Son of Man is)?

**2.** The articular infinitive (with neuter article).
Is commonly the equivalent of an English gerund. Denotes a
process (present tense), an event (aorist tense), or a state
resulting from a prior action (perfect tense).

**a.** In various cases, to express a normal meaning of the case.
Phl. 1:21 (nom., subject of understood verb; substantive
function), τὸ ζῆν Χριστὸς καὶ τὸ ἀποθανεῖν κέρδος, living
is Christ and dying is gain. Lk. 1:9 (gen., object of verb;
purpose function), ἔλαχε τοῦ θυμιᾶσαι, he was selected by
lot to burn (i.e., for the purpose of burning) incense. Ac.
25:11 (acc., object of verb; substantive function), οὐ
παραιτοῦμαι τὸ ἀποθανεῖν.

**b.** Special uses in the genitive case

1) To express purpose. Mt. 2:13, μέλλει γὰρ Ἡρῴδης ζητεῖν
τὸ παιδίον τοῦ ἀπολέσαι αὐτό, for Herod is about to
seek the child for the purpose of destroying him. Mt.
3:13, τοῦ βαπτισθῆναι.

2) Occasionally, to express result distinct from purpose. Ro.
7:3, ἐλευθέρα ἐστὶν ἀπὸ τοῦ νόμου, τοῦ μὴ εἶναι αὐτὴν
μοιχαλίδα, she is free from the law, with the result that
she is not an adulteress. Mt. 21:32, τοῦ πιστεῦσαι.

3) Used as a substantive in various ways

a) As subject. Ac. 27:1, ἐκρίθη τοῦ ἀποπλεῖν ἡμᾶς, it was
decided that we should sail.
b) As object. Ac. 23:20, οἱ Ἰουδαῖοι συνέθεντο τοῦ
ἐρωτῆσαι, the Jews have agreed to request.
c) To limit or explain a noun, verb, or adjective. Lk. 2:6
(limiting a noun), ἐπλήσθησαν αἱ ἡμέραι τοῦ τεκεῖν
αὐτήν, the days of her giving birth (i.e., for her to give
birth) were fulfilled. Lk. 9:51 (limiting a verb), αὐτὸς
τὸ πρόσωπον ἐστήρισεν τοῦ πορεύεσθαι εἰς
Ἰερουσαλήμ, he steadfastly set his face for going (i.e.,
to go) into Jerusalem. Ac. 23:15 (limiting an adjective),
ἕτοιμοι . . . τοῦ ἀνελεῖν αὐτόν.
d) To express indirect discourse and other indirect
statements. Ac. 15:20, ἀλλὰ ἐπιστεῖλαι αὐτοῖς τοῦ
ἀπέχεσθαι τῶν ἀλισγημάτων τῶν εἰδώλων, but to
write to them to abstain from the pollutions of idols
(the direct form would be the imperative mood,
"Abstain from . . ."). Ac. 21:12, παρεκαλοῦμεν . . . τοῦ
μὴ ἀναβαίνειν.

**c.** In prepositional phrases

1) Substantive use, as object of various prepositions, following the regular meaning for the preposition and case used. Jn. 2:24, διὰ τὸ αὐτὸν γινώσκειν πάντας, on account of his knowing (i.e., because he knew) all people. Jn. 1:48, Πρὸ τοῦ σε Φίλιππον φωνῆσαι, before Philip called you. Lk. 2:27, ἐν τῷ εἰσαγαγεῖν τοὺς γονεῖς τὸ παιδίον Ἰησοῦν.

2) Uses with εἰς and the accusative

a) To express purpose. Ro. 4:16, εἰς τὸ εἶναι βεβαίαν τὴν ἐπαγγελίαν, in order that the promise might be guaranteed. Ro. 7:4, εἰς τὸ γενέσθαι ὑμᾶς ἑτέρῳ.

b) Occasionally, to express result distinct from purpose. 1 Th. 2:16, εἰς τὸ ἀναπληρῶσαι αὐτῶν τὰς ἁμαρτίας, resulting in filling up their sins. Ro. 1:20, εἰς τὸ εἶναι αὐτοὺς ἀναπολογήτους.

c) Used as a substantive expression, as the predicate of a verb or to express an indirect statement, or to define or limit a verb, adjective, or noun. Phl. 1:23 (to define a noun), τὴν ἐπιθυμίαν ἔχων εἰς τὸ ἀναλῦσαι, having the desire for departing (i.e., to depart). 1 Th. 4:9 (giving the content of an adjective), ὑμεῖς θεοδίδακτοί ἐστε εἰς τὸ ἀγαπᾶν ἀλλήλους, you are God-taught to love (i.e., that you should love) one another. 2 Th. 2:1-2 (indirect exhortation), ἐρωτῶμεν δὲ ὑμᾶς . . . εἰς τὸ μὴ ταχέως σαλευθῆναι.

**F.** The participle. Bu 163-77; Gr §393-7; DM 220-33

**1.** Uses of the tenses of the participle. Bu 53-72; BF §339

**a.** Present. Bu 54-9

1) Continuing or repeated action (the basic function). Jn. 3:20, πᾶς γὰρ ὁ φαῦλα πράσσων, For everyone who makes a practice of doing evil things. Jn. 3:21, ὁ δὲ ποιῶν τὴν ἀλήθειαν.

2) Action simultaneous to the leading verb. Jn. 1:48, ὄντα ὑπὸ τὴν συκῆν εἶδόν σε, while you were under the fig tree I saw you. Jn. 1:47, ἐρχόμενον.

3) Same action as the leading verb. Jn. 1:32, ἐμαρτύρησεν
'Ιωάννης λέγων, John testified, saying. Jn. 18:40,
ἐκραύγασαν οὖν πάλιν λέγοντες.

4) To identify a person or thing by a characteristic activity or
state, usually translated by a noun in English. Mt.
25:14, παρέδωκεν αὐτοῖς τὰ ὑπάρχοντα αὐτοῦ, he
handed over to them his possessions (the things
belonging to him). Jn. 4:37, ἄλλος ἐστὶν ὁ σπείρων.

**b.** Aorist. Bu 59-70

1) Action anticipated to be completed (at the time indicated
by the context) (the basic function). Jn. 1:33, ὁ πέμψας
με . . . εἶπεν, he who sent me . . . said. Jn. 18:22, εἰπών.

2) Action antecedent to the leading verb. Jn. 9:6, ταῦτα
εἰπὼν ἔπτυσεν χαμαί, after he had said these things he
spat on the ground. Jn. 11:4, ἀκούσας δὲ ὁ 'Ιησοῦς
εἶπεν.

3) Same action as the leading verb. Mt. 27:4, Ἥμαρτον
παραδοὺς αἷμα ἀθῷον, I have sinned in betraying
innocent blood. Mt. 28:5, ἀποκριθεὶς . . . εἶπεν.

**c.** Future (rare). Bu 70-1
Expresses action future to the leading verb. Ac. 8:27, ὃς
ἐληλύθει προσκυνήσων, who had come to worship
(subsequent to coming). He. 3:5, εἰς μαρτύριον τῶν
λαληθησομένων, for a testimony of the things which were
going to be spoken (later). Jn. 6:64, ὁ παραδώσων αὐτόν.
Future action is sometimes expressed by the present participle
of μέλλω with the infinitive of the required verb. Jn. 12:4,
λέγει δὲ 'Ιούδας . . . ὁ μέλλων αὐτὸν παραδιδόναι, Judas,
. . . who was going to betray him, said. Ac. 22:5, ἄξων.
Future action is sometimes expressed by the present
participle--e.g., Jn. 11:3, λέγουσαι, and Ac. 15:5, λέγοντες,
saying (subsequently)--or by the aorist participle--e.g., Ac.
25:13, κατήντησαν εἰς Καισάρειαν ἀσπασάμενοι τὸν
Φῆστον, they arrived in Caesarea greeting Festus (after
they had arrived).

**d.** Perfect. Bu 71-2
Expresses a state resulting from previous action. Jn. 15:25, ὁ
λόγος ὁ . . . γεγραμμένος, the word which stands written.
Jn. 1:6, ἀπεσταλμένος.

**2.** Functions of the participle

**a.** Adjectival

    **1)** Includes all attributive participles

        **a)** Definite restrictive. Jn. 6:50, ὁ ἄρτος ὁ . . . καταβαίνων, the bread which comes down. Jn. 4:11, τὸ ὕδωρ τὸ ζῶν.

        **b)** Indefinite restrictive. Jn. 15:2, πᾶν κλῆμα . . . μὴ φέρον καρπόν, Every branch which does not bear fruit. Jn. 4:10, ὕδωρ ζῶν.

        **c)** Definite non-restrictive. Jn. 7:50, Νικόδημος . . , ὁ ἐλθὼν πρὸς αὐτὸν πρότερον, Nicodemus, who had come to him previously. Lk. 20:27, τινες τῶν Σαδδουκαίων, οἱ [ἀντι]λέγοντες ἀνάστασιν μὴ εἶναι.

        **d)** Indefinite non-restrictive. Jn. 5:2, κολυμβήθρα, ἡ ἐπιλεγομένη Ἑβραϊστὶ Βηθζαθά, πέντε στοὰς ἔχουσα, a pool, which is called in Hebrew Bethzatha, *which has* five porticoes. Jn. 4:14, πηγὴ . . . ἁλλομένου.

*Note*: Restrictive participles may modify an understood noun-- i.e., may be used substantively. Jn. 3:13, ὁ ἐκ τοῦ οὐρανοῦ καταβάς, the one (i.e., the person) having come down from heaven. Jn. 10:21, ταῦτα τὰ ῥήματα οὐκ ἔστιν δαιμονιζομένου, these words are not of (a person) who is demon-possessed.

    **2)** Includes some predicate participles

    **a)** Primary predicates

        **(1)** Participles used as subject complements, modifying the subject. Jn. 18:18, ἦν δὲ καὶ ὁ Πέτρος μετ᾽ αὐτῶν ἑστὼς καὶ θερμαινόμενος, and Peter also was with them, standing and warming himself. Jn. 1:31, ἦλθον ἐγὼ . . . βαπτίζων, I came . . . baptizing. Eph. 1:16, οὐ παύομαι εὐχαριστῶν.
        **(2)** Participles used in periphrastic tense formations. Jn. 3:24, οὔπω γὰρ ἦν βεβλημένος εἰς τὴν φυλακὴν Ἰωάννης, for John had not yet been cast into prison. Lk. 24:13, ἦσαν πορευόμενοι. Lk. 24:32, καιομένη ἦν.

    **b)** Secondary predicates. Participles used as predicate complements, modifying the object of a verb. Jn. 1:29, βλέπει τὸν Ἰησοῦν ἐρχόμενον, he saw Jesus coming. Jn. 1:32, τεθέαμαι τὸ πνεῦμα καταβαῖνον.

**b.** Adverbial
Includes all other predicate participles.
*Note*: Genitive absolute participles are always adverbial.

1) Time. May be translated by an English temporal clause introduced by 'while' (if present tense), 'after' (if aorist tense), 'when,' etc. Jn. 6:59, Ταῦτα εἶπεν . . . διδάσκων, These things he said . . . while he was teaching. Jn. 4:54, ἐλθών.

2) Condition. May be translated by an English conditional clause introduced by 'if', etc. 1 Cor. 11:29, μὴ διακρίνων τὸ σῶμα, if he does not discern the body. Ga. 6:9, μὴ ἐκλυόμενοι.

3) Concession. May be translated by an English concessive clause introduced by 'although', 'even though', 'even if'. Jn. 9:25, τυφλὸς ὤν, although I was blind. Jn. 12:37, αὐτοῦ . . . πεποιηκότος.

4) Cause. May be translated by an English causal clause introduced by 'because', 'for', 'since', etc. Jn. 5:13, ὄχλου ὄντος ἐν τῷ τόπῳ, because a crowd was in the place. Jn. 11:51, ἀρχιερεὺς ὤν.

5) Purpose. May be translated by an English purpose clause introduced by 'in order that', 'in order to', etc., or by an English infinitive of purpose. (*Note*: Future adverbial participles regularly denote purpose.) 2 Cor. 1:23, φειδόμενος ὑμῶν, in order to spare you. Jn. 6:6, πειράζων αὐτόν.

6) Result (as distinct from purpose). May be translated 'resulting in' (*not* 'as a result of'). Mk. 7:13, ἀκυροῦντες τὸν λόγον τοῦ θεοῦ, resulting in nullifying the word of God. Jn. 5:18, ἴσον ἑαυτὸν ποιῶν τῷ θεῷ.

7) Means. Used of the agent or instrument of an action. Mt. 6:27, τίς δὲ ἐξ ὑμῶν μεριμνῶν δύναται . . . , who of you by being anxious is able . . . ? Jn. 20:31, πιστεύοντες.

8) Manner. Ac. 2:13, ἕτεροι δὲ διαχλευάζοντες ἔλεγον, but others mocking (i.e., in a mocking manner) were saying. 1 Cor. 9:26, ὡς οὐκ ἀέρα δέρων.

9) Attendant circumstance. Normally follows the leading verb in word order; normally is present tense. Describes a circumstance as merely accompanying the leading verb, with the sense of "and in addition, this," and

semantically in the same mood as the leading verb. May
seem to be closely related to the participle used as
subject complement or predicate complement--a.2)a)
above--but those are more *descriptive* of the noun
modified, while the participle of attendant circumstance
is merely an *accompanying action* which does not qualify
the action of the leading verb. Jn. 19:5, ἐξῆλθεν . . .
φορῶν τὸν ἀκάνθινον στέφανον, he went outside,
wearing the crown of thorns. Jn. 19:17, βαστάζων
ἑαυτῷ τὸν σταυρὸν ἐξῆλθεν.

10) Coordinate circumstance. Normally precedes the leading
verb in word order; normally aorist tense. Describes an
action coordinate with, prior to, and of the same mood
semantically as the leading verb, although often not
equal in importance with the leading verb. It gives new
information. Its action does not qualify the action of the
leading verb. It may be translated by the same tense and
mood as the leading verb and connected with it by 'and'.
It occurs with any mood: e.g.,
Indicative--Jn. 12:36, ἀπελθὼν ἐκρύβη, he departed and
hid himself.
Subjunctive--Jn. 12:24, ἐὰν μὴ ὁ κόκκος τοῦ σίτου πεσὼν
εἰς τὴν γῆν ἀποθάνῃ, unless the grain of wheat falls
into the ground and dies.
Imperative--Ac. 16:9, Διαβὰς εἰς Μακεδονίαν βοήθησον
ἡμῖν, Come over into Macedonia and help us.
Infinitive--Lk. 11:7, οὐ δύναμαι ἀναστὰς δοῦναί σοι, I am
not able to arise and give to you.
There may be a series of these participles; e.g., Mk. 15:36,
δραμὼν . . . γεμίσας . . . περιθεὶς . . . ἐπότιζεν αὐτόν,
He ran . . . and filled . . . and placed . . . and gave it to
him to drink.

11) Apposition. Same action as the leading verb. Jn. 1:32,
ἐμαρτύρησεν Ἰωάννης λέγων, John testified, saying. Jn.
4:31, λέγοντες.
In some O.T. quotations, the participle stands before the
finite verb and emphasizes the meaning of the verb. Mt.
13:14, βλέποντες βλέψετε, see indeed! He. 6:14, εὐλογῶν
εὐλογήσω.

c. Substantive

The participial phrase functions as a noun clause. Lk. 8:46,
ἐγὼ γὰρ ἔγνων δύναμιν ἐξεληλυθυῖαν ἀπ' ἐμοῦ, for I
know power having gone out (i.e., that power has gone

out) from me. Ac. 8:23, ὁρῶ σε ὄντα (= ὁρῶ ὅτι εἶ). Ac. 7:12, ἀκούσας δὲ ᾽Ιακὼβ ὄντα σιτία (= ὅτι σιτία ἐστίν) εἰς Αἴγυπτον.

## VII. SUMMARY OF CONSTRUCTIONS.

### A. Time. DM 279 ff.

#### 1. Definite time

**a.** Time within which
Genitive case. Jn. 3:2, οὗτος ἦλθεν . . . νυκτός, This man came . . . during the night.

**b.** Point of time

1) Dative case. Jn. 2:1, τῇ ἡμέρᾳ τῇ τρίτῃ, on the third day.

2) ἐν with the dative case. Jn. 1:1, ᾽Εν ἀρχῇ ἦν ὁ λόγος, In the beginning was the Word.

**c.** Extent of time
Accusative case. Jn. 4:40, ἔμεινεν ἐκεῖ δύο ἡμέρας, he remained there for two days.

#### 2. Relative time

**a.** Time prior to the leading verb

1) Prepositional phrase: μετά with the accusative. Jn. 4:43, Μετὰ δὲ τὰς δύο ἡμέρας, And after the two days.

2) Aorist participle. Jn. 16:8, ἐλθὼν ἐκεῖνος ἐλέξει τὸν κόσμον, when that one has come he will reprove the world. Jn. 5:11, ῾Ο ποιήσας με ὑγιῆ . . . εἶπεν, He who (previously) made me well . . . said.

3) Clauses

a) Actual time. Clauses introduced by ὅτε, ὡς ('when', 'while'), etc., with the indicative mood. Jn. 4:45, ὅτε οὖν ἦλθεν εἰς τὴν Γαλιλαίαν, ἐδέξαντο αὐτὸν οἱ Γαλιλαῖοι, then when he came into Galilee, the Galileans received him. Jn. 2:23, ῾Ως δὲ ἦν ἐν τοῖς ῾Ιεροσολύμοις, Now while he was in Jerusalem.

**b)** Contingent time (future possibility or general contingency). Clauses introduced by ὅταν ('when', 'whenever'), etc., with the subjunctive mood. Jn. 4:25, (unrealized future) ὅταν ἔλθῃ ἐκεῖνος, ἀναγγελεῖ ἡμῖν ἅπαντα, when that one comes, he will announce to us all things. Jn. 10:4 (general contingency), ὅταν τὰ ἴδια πάντα ἐκβάλῃ, ἔμπροσθεν αὐτῶν πορεύεται, Whenever he puts forth all his own (sheep), he goes ahead of them.

**b.** Same time as the leading verb

  **1)** Prepositional phrase: ἐν with the dative. Lk. 24:51, ἐν τῷ εὐλογεῖν αὐτὸν αὐτοὺς διέστη ἀπ' αὐτῶν, while he was blessing them he was parted from them.

  **2)** Present participle. Jn. 6:59, Ταῦτα εἶπεν . . . διδάσκων, These things he said . . . while he was teaching. Jn. 3:21, ὁ δὲ ποιῶν τὴν ἀλήθειαν ἔρχεται πρὸς τὸ φῶς, but the one doing the truth comes to the light.

  **3)** Clauses

   **a)** Actual time. Clauses introduced by ἕως, ὡς ('while'), etc. Jn. 9:4, ἡμᾶς δεῖ ἐργάζεσθαι . . . ἕως ἡμέρα ἐστίν, It is necessary for us to be working . . . while it is day.

   **b)** Contingent time. Clauses introduced by ἕως οὗ, ἕως ἄν ('while'), etc., with the subjunctive mood. Mt. 14:22, καὶ προάγειν αὐτὸν εἰς τὸ πέραν, ἕως οὗ ἀπολύσῃ τοὺς ὄχλους, and to precede him to the other side, while he dismissed the crowds. Mk. 6:10, ἐκεῖ μένετε ἕως ἄν ἐξέλθητε ἐκεῖθεν.

**c.** Time subsequent to the leading verb

  **1)** Prepositional phrases

   **a)** ἕως with the genitive case. Lk. 23:44, σκότος ἐγένετο ἐφ' ὅλην τὴν γῆν ἕως ὥρας ἐνάτης, darkness came upon all the earth until the ninth hour.

   **b)** πρό with the genitive case. Jn. 1:48, πρὸ τοῦ σε Φίλιππον φωνῆσαι . . . εἶδόν σε, Before Philip called you . . . I saw you.

   **c)** ἄχρι with the genitive. Ac. 23:1, ἄχρι ταύτης τῆς ἡμέρας, until this day.

2) πρίν or πρὶν ἤ with the infinitive. Jn. 4:49, κατάβηθι πρὶν ἀποθανεῖν τὸ παιδίον μου, come down before my child dies.

3) Future participle, or present participle of μέλλω with an infinitive. Jn. 6:64, ᾔδει . . . ὁ Ἰησοῦς . . . τίς ἐστιν ὁ παραδώσων αὐτόν, Jesus knew . . . who was the one who was going to betray him. Jn. 12:4, λέγει δὲ Ἰούδας . . . ὁ μέλλων αὐτὸν παραδιδόναι, Judas . . . , who was going to betray him, said.

4) Clauses

a) Actual time. Clauses introduced by ἕως, ἄχρι ('until'), etc., with the indicative mood. Jn. 9:18, οὐκ ἐπίστευσαν οὖν οἱ Ἰουδαῖοι . . . ἕως ὅτου ἐφώνησεν τοὺς γονεῖς αὐτοῦ, The Jews therefore did not believe . . . until they had called his parents.

b) Contingent time. Clauses introduced by ἄχρις οὗ ('until'), etc., with the subjunctive mood. 1 Cor. 11:26, τὸν θάνατον τοῦ κυρίου καταγγέλλετε, ἄχρις οὗ ἔλθῃ, you declare the Lord's death until he comes.

B. Cause. DM 274-5; Bu 97-8

1. Prepositional phrases

a. ἀντί with the genitive. Eph. 5:31, ἀντὶ τούτου, Because of this.

b. διά with the accusative. Jn. 2:24, διὰ τὸ αὐτὸν γινώσκειν πάντας, because of his knowing all people.

c. χάριν with the genitive. 1 Jn. 3:12, χάριν τίνος; because of what?

2. Predicate participle. Jn. 5:13, ἐξένευσεν ὄχλου ὄντος ἐν τῷ τόπῳ, he had slipped away because a crowd was in the place.

3. Clauses with γάρ, ὅτι ('for', 'because'), etc. Jn. 7:29, ἐγὼ οἶδα αὐτόν, ὅτι παρ' αὐτοῦ εἰμι, I know him, because I am from him. Jn. 3:19, ἠγάπησαν οἱ ἄνθρωποι μᾶλλον τὸ σκότος ἤ τὸ φῶς, ἦν γὰρ αὐτῶν πονηρὰ τὰ ἔργα, people loved the darkness rather than the light, for their deeds were evil.

Note: ὅτι commonly gives the reason for what immediately precedes, or sometimes for what follows. γάρ always relates to something preceding--a word, clause, or even something implied--and always in the sense of cause, evidence, reason, or explanation, like "for" in English.

## C. Condition. DM 286-91; Gr §383; Bu 100-12

**1.** Participle. Ga. 6:9, θερίσομεν μὴ ἐκλυόμενοι, we shall reap if we do not grow weary.

**2.** Clauses

**a.** Condition of fact: εἰ with the indicative. Conditions which either are or are not true when the statement is made. They relate to either past, present, future, or a general truth. The speaker may or may not believe that the condition is true. May be translated, e.g., "If it is / is not true that . . ." Jn. 20:15, εἰ σὺ ἐβάστασας αὐτόν, If you have carried him away. Mt. 12:28, εἰ δὲ ἐν πνεύματι θεοῦ ἐγὼ ἐκβάλλω τὰ δαιμόνια, If (it is true that) by the Spirit of God I cast out the demons.

**b.** Condition of contingency: ἐάν with the subjunctive. Either a future condition which may or may not become fulfilled, or a general, often-repeated condition when no actual instance is being considered. The speaker may or may not believe that the condition will be fulfilled. May be translated, e.g., "If it should happen that . . ." Jn. 14:3, ἐὰν πορευθῶ καὶ ἑτοιμάσω τόπον ὑμῖν, if I should go and prepare a place for you. Jn. 8:54, Ἐὰν ἐγὼ δοξάσω ἐμαυτόν, If I should glorify myself.

**c.** Hesitant condition: εἰ with the optative. Conditions of fact which are less likely to be true, or conditions of contingency which are less likely to become fulfilled. Ac. 24:19, εἴ τι ἔχοιεν πρὸς ἐμέ, if they should happen to have anything against me. Ac. 27:39, εἰ δύναιντο ἐξῶσαι τὸ πλοῖον, if it might be possible to save the ship.

**d.** Condition contrary to fact: εἰ with the indicative--one of the past tenses in both the conditional clause and the independent clause, and often ἄν in the independent clause. The speaker expresses what he believes is the opposite of the actual situation. Relates to a matter which is already settled. Jn. 5:46, εἰ γὰρ ἐπιστεύετε Μωϋσεῖ, ἐπιστεύετε ἂν ἐμοί, for if you believed Moses, you would believe me. Lk. 7:39, Οὗτος εἰ ἦν προφήτης, ἐγίνωσκεν ἂν τίς καὶ ποταπὴ ἡ γυνὴ ἥτις ἅπτεται αὐτοῦ, This man, if he were a prophet (which I believe he is not), would know who and what sort is the woman who is touching him. Jn. 15:22, εἰ μὴ ἦλθον

καὶ ἐλάλησα αὐτοῖς, ἁμαρτίαν οὐκ εἴχοσαν, If I had not
come and spoken to them (which I did), they would not have
sin.

**D.** Grounds. BC 306-7

εἰ with the indicative. If the speaker has stated his assumption
concerning the truth or falsity of the εἰ clause, or if the
context makes his assumption clear, then and only then the
εἰ clause states the *grounds*, not the condition, and the εἰ
may be translated 'since' as well as 'if'. Ga. 4:7, ὥστε οὐκέτι
εἶ δοῦλος ἀλλὰ υἱός· εἰ δὲ υἱός, καὶ κληρονόμος διὰ θεοῦ,
Therefore you are no longer a slave but a son; and if (since)
you are a son, you are also an heir through God.

**E.** Concession. DM 291-3; Bu 112-6
A condition inadequate for fulfillment, or with a consequence
contrary to expectation. Translated by 'although,' 'even
though,' 'even if,' etc.

**1.** Predicate participle. Jn. 9:25, τυφλὸς ὢν ἄρτι βλέπω, although
I was blind, now I see.

**2.** Clauses

**a.** Concession of fact. Concessions relating to the past, present,
or future, or to a general truth whose truth or falsity is
already settled. εἰ καί or εἰ with the indicative. Lk. 18:4, εἰ
καὶ τὸν θεὸν οὐ φοβοῦμαι, Although I do not fear God. He.
6:9, εἰ καὶ οὕτως λαλοῦμεν, even though we are speaking
thus.

**b.** Concession of contingency. Concessions which may or may not
become fulfilled; the degree of certainty varies. Jn. 11:25,
κἂν ἀποθάνῃ ζήσεται, even if he should die he shall live.
Jn. 10:38, κἂν ἐμοὶ μὴ πιστεύητε, τοῖς ἔργοις πιστεύετε,
even if you do not believe me, believe the works.

**F.** Purpose. Gr §384; DM 282-5; Bu (see index)

**1.** Prepositional phrase: εἰς, sometimes πρός, with the accusative.
Jn. 9:39, εἰς κρίμα, For the purpose of judgment. Ro. 3:26,
πρὸς τὴν ἔνδειξιν τῆς δικαιοσύνης αὐτοῦ, for the purpose of
the demonstration of his righteousness.

**2.** Predicate participle. Jn. 6:6, τοῦτο δὲ ἔλεγεν πειράζων αὐτόν,
But this he was saying for the purpose of testing him.

3. Anarthrous infinitive. Jn. 1:33, ὁ πέμψας με βαπτίζειν, he who
sent me to baptize (i.e., for the purpose of baptizing).

4. Genitive case of the articular infinitive. Mt. 11:1, μετέβη
ἐκεῖθεν τοῦ διδάσκειν καὶ κηρύσσειν, he went away from
there for the purpose of teaching and preaching.

5. Clauses introduced by ἵνα, ὅπως, sometimes μή. Jn. 3:16, ἵνα
πᾶς ὁ πιστεύων εἰς αὐτὸν μὴ ἀπόληται, in order that
everyone who believes in him might not perish. Jn. 11:57,
ὅπως πιάσωσιν αὐτόν, in order that they might seize him.
Mk. 13:36, μὴ . . . εὕρη ὑμᾶς καθεύδοντας, lest . . . he
should (i.e., in order that he may not) find you sleeping.

G. Result. DM 285-6; Bu (see index)

1. ὥστε with the infinitive (twice with the indicative in the N.T.).
This is the regular expression for result in the N.T. 1 Cor.
13:2, κἂν ἔχω πᾶσαν τὴν πίστιν ὥστε ὄρη μεθιστάναι, and if
I should have all faith, with the result that I could remove
mountains.

2. Expressions which commonly express purpose, but which may
express result when the context indicates that the meaning
is result rather than purpose.

a. Prepositional phrase: εἰς with the accusative. Ro. 1:20, εἰς τὸ
εἶναι αὐτοὺς ἀναπολογήτους, with the result that they are
without excuse.

b. Predicate participle. Jn. 5:18, πατέρα ἴδιον ἔλεγεν τὸν θεόν,
ἴσον ἑαυτὸν ποιῶν τῷ θεῷ, he was calling God his own
father, thereby (i.e., as a result he was) making himself
equal to God.

c. Anarthrous infinitive. Rev. 5:5, ἐνίκησεν ὁ λέων ὁ ἐκ τῆς
φυλῆς Ἰούδα, . . . ἀνοῖξαι τὸ βιβλίον, the Lion who is of the
tribe of Judah . . . has conquered, with the result that he
can open the scroll.

d. Genitive case of the articular infinitive. Ro. 7:3, ἐὰν δὲ
ἀποθάνῃ ὁ ἀνήρ, ἐλευθέρα ἐστὶν ἀπὸ τοῦ νόμου, τοῦ μὴ
εἶναι αὐτὴν μοιχαλίδα γενομένην ἀνδρὶ ἑτέρῳ, But if her
husband dies, she is free from the law, resulting in her not
being an adulteress if she becomes another man's (wife).

e. Clauses introduced by ἵνα or ὅπως. Jn. 9:2, τίς ἥμαρτεν, . . .
ἵνα τυφλὸς γεννηθῇ; who sinned, . . . resulting in his being
born blind? Lk. 16:26, μεταξὺ ἡμῶν καὶ ὑμῶν χάσμα μέγα

ἐστήρικται, ὅπως οἱ θέλοντες διαβῆναι ἔνθεν πρὸς ὑμᾶς μὴ δύνωνται, between us and you a great chasm is fixed, with the result that they who wish to pass through from here to you are not able.

**H.** Substantive expressions. DM 293-6

1. Direct discourse. Jn. 3:3, εἶπεν αὐτῷ, Ἀμὴν ἀμὴν . . . , he said to him, "Truly, truly, . . ." Sometimes introduced by ὅτι (untranslated): Jn. 1:20, ὡμολόγησεν ὅτι Ἐγὼ οὐκ εἰμὶ ὁ Χριστός, he confessed, "I am not the Christ."

2. Clauses (not causal) introduced by ὅτι, 'that', the indirect form of a statement whose direct form would be in the *indicative* mood. Take the indicative mood, and the tense which the direct statement would have. Jn. 1:34, μεμαρτύρηκα ὅτι οὗτός ἐστιν ὁ υἱὸς τοῦ θεοῦ, I have testified that this is the Son of God. Jn. 5:15, ἀνήγγειλεν τοῖς Ἰουδαίοις ὅτι Ἰησοῦς ἐστιν ὁ ποιήσας αὐτὸν ὑγιῆ, he announced to the Jews that Jesus was the one who had made him whole (the direct statement would be, "Jesus is the one who has made me whole.").

3. Clauses (not purpose or result) introduced by ἵνα, ὅπως, or μή. Take the subjunctive mood, and the tense which the direct statement would have (occasionally, take the future indicative).

   a. The indirect form of a statement whose direct form would be in a mood other than the indicative. Jn. 4:47, ἠρώτα ἵνα καταβῇ καὶ ἰάσεται αὐτοῦ τὸν υἱόν, he asked that he would come down and heal his son (the direct statement would be, "Come down and heal my son.").

   b. A clause defining, limiting, or giving the content of a noun, adjective, etc. Jn. 1:27, οὐκ εἰμὶ ἄξιος ἵνα λύσω αὐτοῦ τὸν ἱμάντα τοῦ ὑποδήματος, I am not worthy that I should loose the thong of his sandal.

4. Anarthrous infinitive. An alternative for either 2. or 3. above. Jn. 21:25, οὐδ' αὐτὸν οἶμαι τὸν κόσμον χωρήσειν τὰ γραφόμενα βιβλία, I think that not even the world itself would have room for the books which would be written (lit., the world not to be going to have room for). Jn. 4:40, ἠρώτων αὐτὸν μεῖναι παρ' αὐτοῖς, they were asking him to remain with them (the direct statement would be, "Remain with us.").

**5.** Genitive case of the articular infinitive. To define or limit a noun, etc., as with 3. above. Lk. 10:19, δέδωκα ὑμῖν τὴν ἐξουσίαν τοῦ πατεῖν ἐπάνω ὄφεων, I have given you the authority to tread upon serpents.

**6.** Prepositional phrase: εἰς with the accusative. Sometimes as the object of a verb. 2 Th. 2:1-2, Ἐρωτῶμεν . . . εἰς τὸ μὴ ταχέως σαλευθῆναι ὑμᾶς, We ask . . . that you not be quickly shaken. 1 Cor. 15:45, ἐγένετο ὁ πρῶτος ἄνθρωπος Ἀδὰμ εἰς ψυχὴν ζῶσαν, The first man Adam became a living soul.

**7.** Participle. Participial phrase functioning as a noun clause. Lk. 8:46, ἐγὼ γὰρ ἔγνων δύναμιν ἐξεληλυθυῖαν ἀπ᾽ ἐμοῦ, for I know power having gone out (i.e., that power has gone out) from me. Ac. 8:23, εἰς γὰρ χολὴν πικρίας . . . ὁρῶ σε ὄντα, for in the gall of bitterness . . . I see you being (i.e., I see that you are in the gall of bitterness).

**I.** Questions. Ma 170-2

**1.** If prefaced by οὐ, an affirmative reply is expected; if prefaced by μή, a negative reply is expected. However, the reply the questioner expects may or may not be the reply he believes is correct.

**2.** Questions are classified under *each* of the following headings:

**a.** *Real* or *rhetorical*

    **1)** Real: asks for information. Jn. 1:22, εἶπαν οὖν αὐτῷ, Τίς εἶ; Therefore they said to him, "Who are you?"

    **2)** Rhetorical: no answer expected. Ro. 8:31, Τί οὖν ἐροῦμεν πρὸς ταῦτα; What then shall we say to these things?

**b.** *Factual* or *deliberative*

    **1)** Factual: deals with what is either true or false; indicative mood. Jn. 1:38, λέγει αὐτοῖς, Τί ζητεῖτε; he said to them, "What are you seeking?"

    **2)** Deliberative: deals with desirability, possibility, necessity, or obligation; subjunctive mood. Obligation: Mk. 12:14, δῶμεν ἢ μὴ δῶμεν; Should we give or should we not give? Desirability: Ro. 6:1, ἐπιμένωμεν τῇ ἁμαρτίᾳ, Should we continue in sin?

**c.** *Direct* or *indirect*

1) Direct. Jn. 5:6, λέγει αὐτῷ, Θέλεις ὑγιὴς γενέσθαι; he said to him, "Do you want to become well?"

2) Indirect. Jn. 9:21, τίς ἤνοιξεν αὐτοῦ τοὺς ὀφθαλμοὺς ἡμεῖς οὐκ οἴδαμεν, we do not know who opened his eyes.

*Note:* In Acts, εἰ with the optative mood is used as a more hesitant form of an indirect question of fact. Ac. 10:17, διηπόρει ὁ Πέτρος τί ἂν εἴη τὸ ὅραμα ὃ εἶδεν, Peter was perplexed as to what the vision which he had seen might be.

*Note:* Indirect questions preserve the tense, mood, and any interrogative word of the direct form of the question. When the direct form has no interrogative word, the indirect form is introduced by εἰ, 'whether'. εἰ may also introduce a direct question (as ὅτι may introduce direct statements), in which case it is not translated into English.

3. Examples of types of questions

**a.** Jn. 4:12, μὴ σὺ μείζων εἶ τοῦ πατρὸς ἡμῶν 'Ιακώβ; You are not greater than our father Jacob, are you? (Rhetorical, factual, direct, expecting negative reply)

**b.** Lk. 24:26, οὐχὶ ταῦτα ἔδει παθεῖν τὸν Χριστόν, Wasn't it necessary for the Christ to suffer these things? (Rhetorical, factual, direct, expecting affirmative reply)

**c.** Jn. 12:49, αὐτός μοι ἐντολὴν δέδωκεν τί εἴπω, he himself has given me a commandment (as to) what I should say. (Real, deliberative of desirability, indirect form of "What should I say?")

**d.** Jn. 9:25, ἀπεκρίθη . . . , Εἰ ἁμαρτωλός ἐστιν οὐκ οἶδα, He answered . . . , "Whether he is a sinner I do not know." (Real, factual, indirect form of "Is he a sinner?")

**e.** Ro. 6:1, ἐπιμένωμεν τῇ ἁμαρτίᾳ; Should we continue in sin? (Rhetorical, deliberative of desirability, direct)

**f.** Ac. 17:11, ἀνακρίνοντες τὰς γραφὰς εἰ ἔχοι ταῦτα οὕτως, examining the Scriptures (to see) whether these things might be so. (Real, factual, indirect, hesitant)

## VIII. SUGGESTIONS CONCERNING EXEGESIS

**A.** The three basic questions of exegesis, which can be applied to any unit of meaning--word, phrase, clause, sentence, paragraph, etc.

1. What information does it give? (Tells what, who, why, etc.)

2. To what other word, phrase, clause, etc., is it related, and in what way? E.g., may be related to the following clause, giving the condition; may be related to the preceding noun, telling which one; etc.

3. Where is the prominence or emphasis? (This question does not apply to a single word.) E.g., in the sentence, "The disciple saw the Lord," is the emphasis on "disciple," "saw," or "Lord"? In the sentence, "If you ask me, I will go," is the emphasis on the "if" clause or on "I will go"?

**B.** Clues to emphasis or prominence

1. Word order

**a.** Normal (unemphatic) word order is verb / subject / object, or verb / pronoun object / subject. (Word order for clauses with the verb εἰμί is different.) Jn. 2:9, (ὡς δὲ) ἐγεύσατο ὁ ἀρχιτρίκλινος τὸ ὕδωρ. Jn. 2:4, λέγει αὐτῇ ὁ Ἰησοῦς.
*Note*: Words which *must* stand first or in a particular word order are disregarded in determining emphasis.

**b.** Anything which precedes the verb (except for obligatory word order) is generally prominent. Jn. 2:10, Πᾶς ἄνθρωπος πρῶτον τὸν καλὸν οἶνον τίθησιν (both subject and object prominent). Jn. 2:12, μετὰ τοῦτο κατέβη (prepositional phrase emphasized).

**c.** Occasionally, a word placed later than its normal word order is stressed. Phm. 10, παρακαλῶ σε περὶ τοῦ ἐμοῦ τέκνου, ὃν ἐγέννησα ἐν τοῖς δεσμοῖς, Ὀνήσιμον (emphasis on "Onesimus").

**d.** When a word is separated from its modifier, there may be emphasis on the modifier or on both words. He. 2:3, πῶς ἡμεῖς ἐκφευξόμεθα τηλικαύτης ἀμελήσαντες σωτηρίας (emphasizing "so great" and possibly "salvation").

**e.** A genitive preceding the word it modifies (instead of following, which is normal word order) is emphatic. 1 Cor.

3:9, θεοῦ γάρ ἐσμεν συνεργοί· θεοῦ γεώργιον, θεοῦ οἰκοδομή ἐστε (emphasizing "of God").

**f.** ἵνα, ὅπως, or ὅτι clauses standing first in word order are emphatic. (Clauses with ὅτε, ὅταν, εἰ, or ἐάν normally stand first, without emphasis.)

**2. Emphatic words**

**a.** The nominative pronouns ἐγώ, σύ, ἡμεῖς, ὑμεῖς.

**b.** The possessive adjectives ἐμός, σός, ἡμέτερος, ὑμέτερος, ἴδιος.

**c.** Enclitics accented when accent is not required by rules of accent.

**d.** Forms of αὐτός used as intensive pronouns or as emphatic 3rd person nominative pronouns. Jn. 2:24, αὐτὸς δὲ Ἰησοῦς, But Jesus himself. Jn. 17:8, αὐτοὶ ἔλαβον, they (emphatic) have received.

**e.** The definite article in the nominative case without a substantive, with μέν or δέ. Ac. 17:32, οἱ μὲν ἐχλεύαζον, οἱ δὲ εἶπαν, some mocked, but others said.
In narrative, the article with δέ indicates a change of speaker. Jn. 4:31-2, ἠρώτων αὐτὸν οἱ μαθηταὶ . . . . ὁ δὲ εἶπεν αὐτοῖς, the disciples were asking him . . . . but he said to them.

**f.** οὗτος and ἐκεῖνος sometimes indicate emphasis. Ac. 1:11, οὗτος ὁ Ἰησοῦς, this Jesus. The emphasis may be derogatory: Ac. 7:40, ὁ γὰρ Μωϋσῆς οὗτος, for this Moses.

**C.** Suggestions concerning procedure

**1. Dependent clauses**

**a.** A *noun* clause tells "what." Introduced by ὅτι, ἵνα, ὅπως, etc. Direct quotations are also noun clauses in relation to any introductory clause. Jn. 2:22, ἐμνήσθησαν οἱ μαθηταὶ αὐτοῦ ὅτι τοῦτο ἔλεγεν, his disciples remembered that he had said this. Jn. 4:47, ἠρώτα ἵνα καταβῇ καὶ ἰάσεται αὐτοῦ τὸν υἱόν, he was asking that he come down and heal his son.

**b.** An *adjectival* clause tells "which one" and similar ideas. Commonly introduced by relative pronouns or relative adjectives. Jn. 1:26, μέσος ὑμῶν ἔστηκεν ὃν ὑμεῖς οὐκ

οἴδατε, in the midst of you stands he whom you do not
know. Mk. 6:56, ὅσοι ἂν ἥψαντο αὐτοῦ ἐσῴζοντο, as many
as touched him were made well.

    **c.** An *adverbial* clause tells when, where, how, why, purpose,
result, condition, etc. Introduced by subordinate
conjunctions, relative adverbs, etc. Jn. 17:12, ὅτε ἤμην μετ'
αὐτῶν ἐγὼ ἐτήρουν αὐτούς, When I was with them I was
keeping them. Jn. 8:21, ὅπου ἐγὼ ὑπάγω ὑμεῖς οὐ δύνασθε
ἐλθεῖν, where I am going you are not able to come. Lk.
23:55, ἐθεάσαντο τὸ μνημεῖον καὶ ὡς ἐτέθη τὸ σῶμα
αὐτοῦ, they beheld the tomb and how his body was placed.

**2.** An *independent* clause may be introduced by a conjunction of
addition or contrast--e.g., καί, δέ, ἀλλά ('and', 'but',
'nevertheless')--or may have no introductory word.

**3.** Nouns
    What is the use of its case?
    What is the significance of the presence or absence of the
        article?

**4.** Pronouns
    What is its antecedent--i.e., to what word does it refer?
    What type of pronoun is it, and what therefore is its meaning?

**5.** Adjectives and participles
    What does it modify?
    Is it in attributive or predicate position, and what therefore is
        its meaning?

**6.** Prepositional phrases
    What does the phrase modify?
    What is the meaning of the preposition, considering the case of
        its object?

**7.** Verbs
    What is the use of its mood; or, if it is a participle or infinitive,
        what is its function?
    What is the use of its tense?

**8.** Words
    Investigate the background meaning, even though this
        meaning may have been modified in the course of time.
    Determine the significance of any prefixes or suffixes.
    Pay attention to agreement in gender (e.g., τοῦτο in Eph. 2:8),
        in number (e.g., οὖ in He. 12:14), and in case (e.g.,
        ποιμένα in He. 13:20).

**D.** Special notes on indirect statements

1. The indirect form of direct discourse and other direct statements in the *indicative* mood is expressed either a) by ὅτι and the indicative mood or b) by the infinitive. Jn. 1:34, μεμαρτύρηκα ὅτι οὗτός ἐστιν ὁ υἱὸς τοῦ θεοῦ, I have testified that this is the Son of God. Lk. 11:18, λέγετε ἐν Βεελζεβοὺλ ἐκβάλλειν με τὰ δαιμόνια, you say by Beelzebul me to cast out the demons--i.e., you say that by Beelzebul I cast out the demons.

2. The indirect form of direct discourse and other direct statements in moods other than the indicative is expressed either a) by ἵνα (occasionally ὅπως) and the subjunctive mood or b) by the infinitive. Jn. 4:47, ἠρώτα ἵνα καταβῇ καὶ ἰάσηται αὐτοῦ τὸν υἱόν, he was asking that he come down and heal his son (direct discourse, "Come down and heal my son"). Jn. 4:40, ἠρώτων αὐτὸν μεῖναι παρ' αὐτοῖς, they were asking him to remain with them (direct discourse, "Remain with us").

3. An indirect question is introduced by the same interrogative word as the direct question. Jn. 2:25, ἐγίνωσκεν τί ἦν ἐν τῷ ἀνθρώπῳ, he knew what was in man--i.e., he knew (the answer to the question,) "What is in man?" Lk. 17:20, Ἐπερωτηθεὶς . . . πότε ἔρχεται ἡ βασιλεία τοῦ θεοῦ, Having been asked . . . when the kingdom of God was coming. (The direct question would be, "When is the kingdom of God coming?")
   If the direct question has no interrogative word, the indirect form is introduced by εἰ, 'whether'.

4. The indirect form of questions and of other statements retains the tense of the direct form. Jn. 2:22, ἐμνήσθησαν οἱ μαθηταὶ αὐτοῦ ὅτι τοῦτο ἔλεγεν, his disciples remembered that he had said this (direct statement, "He was saying this"). Jn. 4:1, ἔγνω ὁ Ἰησοῦς ὅτι ἤκουσαν οἱ Φαρισαῖοι ὅτι Ἰησοῦς πλείονας μαθητὰς ποιεῖ καὶ βαπτίζει ἢ Ἰωάννης, Jesus knew that the Pharisees had heard that Jesus was making and baptizing more disciples than John (direct form, "The Pharisees have heard, 'Jesus is making and baptizing more disciples than John' ").

**E.** Special notes on two important connectives

1. γάρ, 'for' (postpositive--cannot stand first in its clause). Always refers to something preceding (like "for" in English), never to something following. Always introduces a dependent clause expressing some form of reason; never is merely the

equivalent of "but," "however," etc., introducing an independent clause.

**a.** Reason for what precedes. Mt. 1:21, καλέσεις τὸ ὄνομα αὐτοῦ Ἰησοῦν, αὐτὸς γὰρ σώσει τὸν λαὸν αὐτοῦ ἀπὸ τῶν ἁμαρτιῶν αὐτῶν, you shall call his name Jesus, for he will save his people from their sins.

**b.** Grounds or basis for what precedes. Lk. 18:31-32, τελεσθήσεται πάντα τὰ γεγραμμένα διὰ τῶν προφητῶν τῷ υἱῷ τοῦ ἀνθρώπου· παραδοθήσεται γὰρ τοῖς ἔθνεσιν, all the things written through the prophets will be completed to the Son of Man; for he will be handed over to the Gentiles.

**c.** Reason or motivation for a preceding exhortation. Mk. 13:33, βλέπετε, ἀγρυπνεῖτε· οὐκ οἴδατε γὰρ πότε ὁ καιρός ἐστιν, Take heed, be watchful; for you do not know when the time is.

**d.** Explanatory, giving background information. Lk. 11:29-30, Ἡ γενεὰ αὕτη . . . σημεῖον ζητεῖ, καὶ σημεῖον οὐ δοθήσεται αὐτῇ εἰ μὴ τὸ σημεῖον Ἰωνᾶ. καθὼς γὰρ ἐγένετο Ἰωνᾶς τοῖς Νινευΐταις σημεῖον, οὕτως ἔσται καὶ ὁ υἱὸς τοῦ ἀνθρώπου τῇ γενεᾷ ταύτῃ, This generation seeks a sign, and a sign will not be given to it except the sign of Jonah; for just as Jonah became a sign to the Ninevites, so shall the Son of Man be a sign to this generation.

**e.** The reason for something implied but not directly stated in what precedes. Jn. 9:30, ἀπεκρίθη ὁ ἄνθρωπος καὶ εἶπεν αὐτοῖς, Ἐν τούτῳ γὰρ τὸ θαυμαστόν ἐστιν, the man answered and said to them, "(I am surprised at what you have said,) for this is a remarkable thing."

**2.** εἰ, 'if', 'whether'.

**a.** Condition of fact, with the indicative mood. Jn. 8:46, εἰ ἀλήθειαν λέγω, διὰ τί ὑμεῖς οὐ πιστεύετέ μοι; if I am saying the truth, why do you not believe me?

**b.** More tentative condition, with the optative mood. 1 Pe. 3:17, εἰ θέλοι τὸ θέλημα τοῦ θεοῦ, if the will of God perchance wills.

**c.** Grounds (only when the writer has already acknowledged that the condition is true or false). 1 Jn. 4:10-11, ἐν τούτῳ ἐστὶν ἡ ἀγάπη, οὐχ ὅτι ἡμεῖς ἠγαπήκαμεν τὸν θεόν, ἀλλ' ὅτι αὐτὸς ἠγάπησεν ἡμᾶς . . . . Ἀγαπητοί, εἰ οὕτως ὁ θεὸς ἠγάπησεν ἡμᾶς . . . , In this is love, not that we loved God, but that he loved us . . . . Beloved, if (since) God thus loved us . . . .

**d.** Condition contrary to fact. Mt. 23:30, Εἰ ἤμεθα ἐν ταῖς ἡμέραις τῶν πατέρων ἡμῶν, οὐκ ἂν ἤμεθα αὐτῶν κοινωνοὶ ἐν τῷ αἵματι τῶν προφητῶν, If we had been in the days of our fathers, we would not have been partakers with them in the blood of the prophets.

**e.** Concession of fact. Lk. 18:4-5, Εἰ καὶ τὸν θεὸν οὐ φοβοῦμαι οὐδὲ ἄνθρωπον ἐντρέπομαι, . . . ἐκδικήσω αὐτήν, Even though I do not fear God nor respect man . . . . I will vindicate her.

**f.** Indirect question (when the direct question has no interrogative introductory word). Lk. 23:6, ἐπηρώτησεν εἰ ὁ ἄνθρωπος Γαλιλαῖός ἐστιν, he asked whether the man was a Galilean (direct form, "Is the man a Galilean?").

**g.** Direct question (εἰ is not translated). Mt. 12:10, ἐπηρώτησαν αὐτὸν λέγοντες, Εἰ ἔξεστιν τοῖς σάββασιν θεραπεῦσαι; they asked him saying, "Is it lawful to heal on the Sabbath?"

# Scripture Index